KU-073-247

THE DINOSAUR MAN

Also by Susan Baur

Hypochondria: Woeful Imaginings

THE
DINOSAUR
MAN

---

*Tales of Madness and Enchantment
from the Back Ward*

SUSAN BAUR

HarperPerennial
A Division of HarperCollinsPublishers
An Edward Burlingame Book

A hardcover edition of this book was published in 1991 by HarperCollins
Publishers.

THE DINOSAUR MAN. Copyright © 1991 by Susan Baur. All rights reserved. Printed
in the United States of America. No part of this book may be used or reproduced
in any manner whatsoever without written permission except in the case of brief
quotations embodied in critical articles and reviews. For information address
HarperCollins Publishers, Inc., 10 East 53rd Street, New York, NY 10022.

HarperCollins books may be purchased for educational, business, or sales
promotional use. For information, please call or write: Special Markets
Department, HarperCollins Publishers, Inc., 10 East 53rd Street, New York,
NY 10022. Telephone: (212) 207-7528; Fax: (212) 207-7222.

First HarperPerennial edition published 1992.

Designed by C. Linda Dingler

The Library of Congress has catalogued the hardcover edition as follows:

Baur, Susan.
    The dinosaur man : tales of madness and enchantment from the back
ward / Susan Baur. — 1st ed.
        p.   cm.
    "Edward Burlingame books."
    ISBN 0-06-016538-3
    1. Schizophrenics—Case studies.   I. Title.
RC514.B375   1991
616.89'82—dc20   90-55948

ISBN 0-06-098104-0 (pbk.)
92 93 94 95 96 CC/RRD 10 9 8 7 6 5 4 3 2 1

For Domenic

CONTENTS

THE DINOSAUR MAN

The observations and characteristics which I describe in *The Dinosaur Man* are based on my actual experiences.

However, the details of various experiences and various places have been changed, and at times combined, to create for this book a representative but fictitious place, Mountain Valley Hospital. Similarly, all names are fictitious and details such as physical traits and specific life experiences have been changed and combined to disguise, and protect, the identity of individuals.

Any similarity to real individuals or places arises from the commonality of experiences of people who suffer from mental illness and of the places where they are treated.

DR. SUSAN BAUR
February 1991

Introduction

For under the language to which we have been listening all our lives, a new, a more profound language . . . offers itself. It is what they call poetry. . . . [And] it is that, we realize, which beyond all they have been saying is what they have been trying to say.

WILLIAM CARLOS WILLIAMS,
"The Practice," in *The Doctor Stories*

When the famous poet and physician William Carlos Williams met a new patient, he reported that the hunt was on. His excitement became intense, the urge to write unbearable. With each individual he was off again on a race against time and against the essential separateness of human beings. Could the patient even begin to put his story into words? Could the doctor hear well enough to catch the underlying song? If they succeeded, they produced poetry as well as good treatment. If they did not, then what was tragic and enduring in life remained hidden from both.

For the past nine years I have worked in places where the essential separateness of individuals is particularly obvious. I have

1

begun the day with men and women who believe themselves to be Robert E. Lee or God the Father and counseled others who shake with the expectation of torture. At the end of the day it is not unusual for me still to say good-bye to a man who believes himself to be a foam-rubber robot and to another who has cut off the heads of stuffed animals and now cries when he hears the voices of his children telling him to be good. In more concrete terms, I have worked in mental hospitals on wards populated by schizophrenics, manic-depressives, and the deeply depressed, and I have worked in clinics for outpatients suffering from a wide range of troubles and compulsions.

Early in my career I had a relatively clear idea of what I was supposed to do in these settings. In one hospital, for example, the task at hand was to transform an old-fashioned ward into an experimental one, where a treatment known as behavior modification would be used to train the seriously and persistently mentally ill in the skills needed for independent living. The goal was to introduce a pervasive system of rewards and punishments that would encourage chronic patients to say please and thank you, wear socks, take their antipsychotic medications, keep their flies zipped up, and in a dozen other ways conform to our visible standards of sanity. Thus rehabilitated, the reasoning went, they would move into foster homes and would have a better chance of fitting into the community than would patients who kept to their eccentric ways.

With outpatients, my job was different, but here again the goals were fairly clear. I worked with these reasonable, uncomfortable people to try to understand what had gone wrong and to support their efforts to move ahead. It took no leap of imagination to understand the stories I heard of unexpected bereavement or repeated abuse, and as I listened to the bitterness of a man who was reconstructing the Maginot Line around his suburban home or to the frustration of a newly paraplegic baker whose wife of twenty-five years no longer wanted sex every night, I could see that it was not grief that brought these people to me, but rather their sense of being immobilized. They seemed to be fighting against themselves or at least against some frightened, less confident part of themselves that was given to betrayal. Initially, I believed that these intimate civil wars constituted the crux of their problems and that broader issues of family needs and social pressures could be treated separately and by someone else.

As time passed, however, my objectives became less clear. Among chronically ill patients who had lived for ten or twenty years on the back wards, for example, few seemed to want to learn what I was supposed to teach them, and even those willing to modify their behavior in order to leave the hospital were not captivated by learning how to ask directions to the bus station or how to start a conversation. These weren't their goals, and our mismatched expectations fostered fairly superficial exchanges.

With the outpatients, too, I found myself questioning the goals of therapy. For one thing, whose goals were actually being pursued? The individuals'? Or, in some cases, was I again being asked to teach my clients how to get along better in society—how to complain less, disturb others less, and cost taxpayers less? Without realizing how much these questions disturbed me, I moved away from the role of teacher and became instead, or in addition, a follower. What was a small, sharp-eyed man really asking for when he showed me his vicious drawings of women with pointed teeth and barbed-wire jewelry, then let me hold the rag doll he cared for with obvious tenderness? What did the man with the mechanical brain and the pressure brain hope for when he gave me the gift of the holy green light?

This shift in objectives, from persuading patients to get a job or speak more clearly to actively listening to whatever they had to say, encouraged a different kind of relationship. As the "daughter" of a man who believed himself to be a Nicodemosaurus, for example, I became a student whose job it was to learn from the expert whatever I could about this schizophrenic's world. For another patient I became something of an auxiliary memory, holding and reinforcing the few stories he could remember of a happier time. For many I was simply a witness. In all instances, I accepted their aliases, their ideas, their rules (not mine) of communication, and, like Williams, I was rewarded by being transported. "I lost myself in the very properties of their minds."

Thus over time I became increasingly familiar with the private thoughts of the moderately troubled and grievously ill, and with this familiarity came respect. I was amazed by their bravery and persistence. I was delighted by the ingenious ways in which all of them crafted reality into the shields or canes or costumes they needed to survive.

It is with regret, then, that I have disguised people and places who deserve to take credit directly for what they have endured and accomplished. Unfortunately, the opprobrium attached to mental illness is still such that patients and institutions alike need the protection of anonymity. Consequently, identifying information has been changed. Consistent with these alterations, I have gathered cases from hospitals, agencies, and clinics and placed them together in a representative complex that I am calling Mountain Valley Hospital and in an ordinary town named Hillsdale. Similarly and where necessary, I have gathered compatible idiosyncrasies from several patients and combined them to make a single identity.

It is a curious business, this disguising of individuals, and at first I thought that my cases would lose something with every substitution that confidentiality required me to make. What I found, however, is that the process of characterization is not so different from therapy itself. Both represent attempts to understand the deep emotional structure of real people living real lives, and both are mirrors in which individuals can see what they are ready to see. With or without the label of *mentally ill*, each person who sees himself in these pages will be correct.

When I think of the places that, together, I am calling Mountain Valley Hospital, I think of spring. Perhaps it is because I can still remember driving in through various main gates at that time of year and seeing a dozen or so brick buildings sprawled like patients on the grassy lawns. Ahead of me there was always an Administration Building, and along both sides of whatever drive

I was on, there were boxwood hedges or ornamental trees. In the Mountain Valley complex where these stories now reside, steep-roofed buildings climbed partway up a narrow valley on either side of a lozenge-shaped drive. Below and to the south lay the old mill town of Hillsdale. Above and to the north the hospital grounds rose to meet steep fields behind which stood a forest of evergreens.

At Mountain Valley there were essentially two populations, outpatients and inpatients, and the latter were subdivided into "acutes" and "chronics." By and large, outpatients at Mountain Valley were indistinguishable from visitors or staff, but inpatients were easier to spot. The boisterous acutes often arrived in an extremely distraught state, with terrified bursts of singing or laughter punctuating their war-torn silences. After they had been stabilized with medications, however, they were free to wander across the wide lawns, sit by the TV, or play cards in the activities room. Most of these patients tried to look as if they had wandered into Mountain Valley by mistake and were on their way to someplace else. They never really became part of the hospital community, and the lucky ones kept a foreignness about them that marked them as outsiders. In a month or two such patients were back in the community.

Chronics, on the other hand, had settled in, and these patients measured their time at Mountain Valley in years or even decades. They were at home here, yet the quality that identified them as mental patients more than any other was, paradoxically, their air of homelessness. They seemed disconnected from their surroundings on several levels. For one thing, they dressed with an alarming insouciance. Men commonly wore two or three shirts apiece, and women roped themselves into dresses that earlier had served as circus tents. One woman powdered her hair, which then exploded in small dust storms whenever she got excited, and a clean-shaven, sharp-eyed man grew a scraggly goatee from his Adam's apple. Occasionally these patients would lie down in the corridors, many talked to themselves, and most declined on a regular basis to acknowledge the presence of others.

Chronic patients also seemed to have lost a certain amount

of contact with their own bodies. A few ate all the time and became enormously fat. More apparently forgot to eat and were scrawny. Almost all smoked until their fingers turned yellow. They seemed unaware that smoking caused their constant coughing or that a half-inch butt was too hot to hold.

Many of the chronic patients—and all of those eager to "elope"—were housed on locked wards at the back of the hospital grounds. Here they were fed in small dining halls and bedded down each night in rooms or open dormitories. From here they were escorted in listless, shuffling groups to the gym or the arts and crafts room.

When chronic patients earned "full privileges" by showing that they would reliably return to their wards for medications and would fulfill other obligations, they too had the run of the grounds. Then they would roam through the halls or sit in the back corner of the hospital canteen.

I remember leaving a lab one afternoon, having failed to convince a rotund patient that a memory test would not poison him. On my way out I passed a familiar patient who was festooned with optical devices. I had seen him before, sitting as he was now, bolt upright on the stone steps of the building. Three or four pairs of glasses protruded from the pockets of his suit coat, binoculars hung from his neck, and a monocle in his right eye was attached to one of his buttons by some fifty or sixty feet of tangled string. What impressed me on this particular afternoon was the man's ability to ignore the commotion that was going on around him.

From one side, a short, wizened old woman was telling him— as indeed she told everyone she encountered—what she honestly thought of the hospital's creamed chipped beef. "The goddamned stuff is worse than stinking shit!" she screamed in his face, and from where I was standing I could see the sunlight sparkle on the saliva that sprayed from her mouth. "Creamed chipped shit!" she screeched at this immovable statue of a man.

On his other side, a rather shapeless woman with a scarf around her head and a large handbag had settled onto the step.

6

"Hello, Leonard," she said warmly to someone I couldn't see. "I mean, oh dear, *Bernie.* It's you."

I moved to get a better view and found that she was holding a powdery compact in her hand and smiling at her own reflection.

Leonard? I thought to myself. Bernie? Reflections, magnifications, chipped beef? What, I wondered, would persuade these people to leave their exotic worlds and enter mine for even a few minutes each day? What did I have to offer?

As I was getting used to moving among the seriously mentally ill, I also began to connect specific illnesses such as schizophrenia or Korsakoff's syndrome with the flamboyantly unusual activities I saw going on around me. A typical ward in Mountain Valley housed patients with a variety of diagnoses. The most common illness was the schizophrenias, which include paranoid schizophrenia, with its persecutory or grandiose delusions, catatonic schizophrenia, with its bizarre postures or almost complete lack of movement, and the disorganized or undifferentiated schizophrenias, characterized respectively by incoherence and grossly disorganized behavior.*

Contrary to the popular conception of schizophrenia, none of these patients had a split personality, but all suffered from persistent psychotic symptoms such as delusions and auditory hallucinations which made it difficult for them to know what was real and what was imaginary much of the time. "My brain plays tricks on me!" I heard a patient say with passionate anger. "You don't know about betrayal until your own brain lets you down."

Less common at Mountain Valley were cases of what is now called major depressive syndrome (depression) and bipolar disorder (manic depression). It was difficult to spot the former on the grounds because they had so little energy that they rarely left the wards, but the manics strode up and down the drive under the ornamental trees rattling off both sides of a heated debate. One

---

*The National Alliance for the Mentally Ill estimates that some 1.6 million Americans suffer from schizophrenia. More than half a million of these individuals will spend a great deal of their lives in hospitals like Mountain Valley, where they make up the overwhelming majority of patients.

great barrel-chested man used to strip off his shirt as if getting ready for a fight. Another, a walleyed scarecrow, used to "preach" with wildly stabbing gestures, which he insisted was his way of reading "Coptic braille."

Less common still than patients with mood disorders were those who suffered from dementias caused, for example, by excessive drinking (Korsakoff's syndrome), by an illness such as Huntington's chorea, or by some unidentified organic process. Very occasionally the hospital census included a boxer who had taken too many punches to the head.

In a place like Mountain Valley, the bulk of the outpatients were far less seriously ill. Some hung around the hospital all day, but I got the impression that most drove in for an hour of therapy, then returned to a job or a family. The most common diagnoses in the outpatient clinics were the mood disorders related to anxiety and depression. Personality disorders, such as histrionic, antisocial, or dependent, were also treated, although these deeply ingrained patterns of living do not yield easily to anything less than years of therapy. The clinic also saw patients with posttraumatic stress disorder, a harrowing malady that first came to public attention after the Vietnam War but has subsequently been shown to affect many victims of childhood abuse as well.

One afternoon, before starting on the inpatient unit that I am calling Ward 9-2-D, I remember walking over to the Administration Building to pick up my passkeys. It was a hot day in August, and the trees along the drive drowsed in the summer sun. In the fields, islands of yellow hawkweed stood stranded in the high grass. Not a leaf or a blade moved. I found the security office and over the whir of fans asked for the keys.

Returning to the back of the building, I bought myself an iced tea in the hospital canteen and set about attaching the keys to my key ring. At the corner tables were regulars from the locked wards, and I already recognized a loud man with curiously yellow eyes and also a small, silent individual who wore a plastic hockey helmet. In the center of the canteen sat a few white-coated psychiatry residents, and at the table across from mine were a group of nurses.

It suddenly occurred to me that no one I'd seen so far at Mountain Valley wore much jewelry except for keys, and that these jangling charms were the real symbol of power, the badge of the insider. With them you could let yourself in and you could let yourself out.

This power, I noted, looking around me, was displayed discreetly by the residents, whose big symbol was the stethoscope, and very obviously by the janitors, who boasted two or even three rings hanging off their belts. But it was the nurses across from me who really "wore" their keys. One displayed hers on the end of a long, beaded fob that clipped to her belt loop. The others wore theirs on colorful plastic bracelets that looked like miniature Slinkies. The keys themselves were capped by plastic covers of different colors, which presumably distinguished one from another. Charge nurses, I knew, were required to wear the most precious of all the keys—the one that opened the medicine closet, the arsenal—around their necks. For safety's sake, no other necklaces were allowed on the wards.

As I left the canteen, I pocketed my only moderately powerful keys and thought back to a conversation I had held earlier in the day with another newcomer. She had asked me why I wanted to "do inpatient" rather than work in outpatient clinics with a more rewarding clientele. At least, she said, I might have tried for an acute ward, where there was some hope that patients would recover. I think I agreed with her then, although now it is difficult to remember. I may have said that I was curious to know how the wraiths of Mountain Valley, whom I had seen staggering through their uncommon worlds, managed to construct lives for themselves from so improbable a collection of thoughts and emotions. Or I may have said I had simply been assigned to 9-2-D. In either case, I'm sure I did not know enough to tell her that I wanted to see how far my understanding would take me into the haunted lives of the seriously ill.

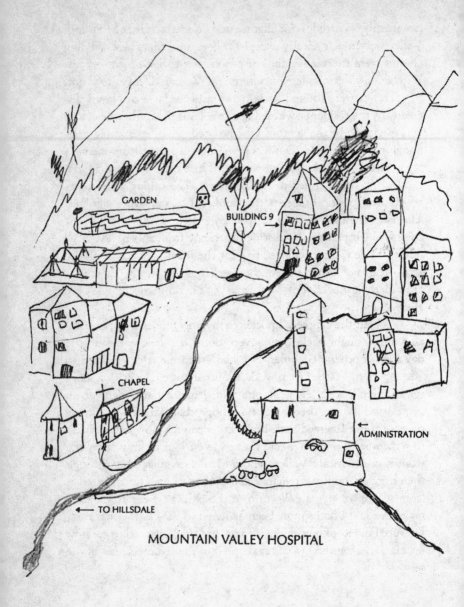

ON THE WARD

The Dinosaur Man

Those who really try to understand human action never limit themselves to psychology.

ERNEST BECKER

When I was assigned to care for a man who was routinely described by clinicians as the craziest human being they had ever met, I did not expect to be dealing with a dinosaur. However, according to Maurice Nouvelle (for such was this dinosaur-schizophrenic's name), this is exactly what happened. He insists that our story began 100 million years ago and that its cycles of fractures and mendings, sadness and sweetness, continue even now to turn as endlessly as the seasons and with the seasons' same disregard for whom they affect. In my more conventional terms, the story began on a hot day in August, as my new keys jangled in a lock, a wooden door swung open, and I stared down the pink-tiled corridor of 9-2-D.

"This is one of the oldest chronic wards at Mountain Valley," said the nurse who met me at the door. And with that I walked onto a ward. I entered an asylum.

Looking down the long corridor with museum prints screwed to the walls far above eye level, I could see a dozen or so men pacing up and down and another half dozen crouched against the wall. The men's average age, I guessed, was about forty-five, and, from the disheveled look of their clothes and the distraction in their eyes, I surmised that none was actively preparing to be released.

"Hello, Doctor," said a towering skeleton of a man. "My name is Billy Mark, a tall man and a good man."

"I don't suppose," chimed in his very short companion, as he fanned away at the heavy smell of cigarettes and age that enveloped us all that hot afternoon, "I don't suppose she knows the difference between Catholic Girls' School anatomy and Catholic Boys' School anatomy."

"I don't suppose she says her rosary," said another, sailing by with beads hanging from his neck and entwined about both hands.

Abruptly all twenty-four patients on the ward turned from their pressing fantasies and, at the sound of "Cigarette call!" shouted by one of the aides, shuffled into line outside a large closet that opened off the main corridor. From here each was given a single cigarette, a ritual that, I soon learned, was repeated on the hour.

It was in this slouching line of castaways that I first saw Mr. Nouvelle. A slight man with a halo of gray hair radiating from his head, he was dressed in a peculiar kind of uniform that seemed made up of a blue security-guard shirt worn over army fatigues. Arcane scribbling had been drawn over one shoulder with colored markers, and a broad, badly spotted tie was held in place with a university tie tack. Several strands of packing twine ran around his neck and disappeared down the front of his shirt; these, I learned later, held his religious medals. I was told that this fifty-six-year-old paranoid schizophrenic considered himself to be God the Father, Inspector General, Howitzer Bombardier, and the renowned conductor Maestro Superbo. I was told, moreover, that he had spent his entire adult life in mental institutions and was so persistently delusional that routine information, such as the names of brothers and sisters, was missing from his record. Because he could not allow anyone to understand him, he could not be reached, much less helped.

For several months Mr. Nouvelle retained his status as complete enigma by avoiding all contact with me except staring. With his hazel eyes considerably magnified by thick, dust-speckled glasses and his pupils often reduced to the size of pinholes by intense emotion, he would peer at me as he glided into the dayroom, there to sit wrapped in his own thoughts, pawing distractedly at the floor.

I cannot remember just what it was that first drew me to Mr. Nouvelle, but it may have been the quality of his preoccupation. Many of the patients on 9-2-D seemed heavily sedated, others simply mindless, but Mr. Nouvelle's disconcertingly intense stare and bizarre gestures suggested that he was actively engaged in private negotiations of a complex and pressing nature. He seemed to be thinking very hard about something.

During my first months on the ward, I did not have a great deal of time to think about what might be on Mr. Nouvelle's mind. I was trying to get my bearings on 9-2-D, which was a great H-shaped ward with dormitories and a dayroom making up one side of the H and offices and meeting rooms making up the other. A glassed-in nurses' station was strategically located between the two so that those on duty could see along both corridors. I was also meeting the hospital staff and learning about the hierarchy that ranked us, in a not undisputed sequence, from psychiatrists at the top, through psychologists, nurses, and social workers, to mental-health aides at the bottom. Above all, I was trying to discover what activities made up a typical day and week for the patients.

I accompanied patients to occupational therapy (OT), recreational therapy (RT), community issues (CI), and all the other places in the hospital labeled with initials. In OT, for example, I watched as patients traced and colored maple leaves in anticipation of fall, and I watched as each according to his or her ingenuity found ways to slip out for water and a cigarette. The really clever ones dodged into the Annex to stir themselves awake with a can of Coke.

Caffeine and nicotine, I gathered, were used to counteract the sedative effects of medications.

Mr. Nouvelle was particularly fond of Coke. From Thursday to Monday—as long as his weekly allowance lasted—I would see him drink four or five cans a day. From Monday through Wednesday, however, he only pretended to drink. He would raise and lower an invisible can, slurp an invisible liquid, then cross himself repeatedly. No one knew why.

After morning activities, almost all the patients at Mountain Valley returned to their wards for "noon meds." The privileged patients then sauntered off to the mess hall, while others, who needed more supervision, waited for the food carts with their covered trays to rattle off the freight elevators and onto the wards.

After lunch there was a slack period when the dormitories were unlocked and the patients allowed to nap. It was quiet on the ward then, and I could sometimes hear the soft crackling of the plastic mattress covers as the patients turned or shifted. Then off to OT or RT went all the patients at one o'clock, and back onto the ward they all came at four. Thus several times a day a hundred or more patients sloshed on and off the wards as regularly as the tides. The staff was fond of saying that this structured regime anchored them in "the real world." However, the repetitiveness also had the effect of running the days and weeks together into a long blur, and many patients were hard-pressed to remember what day or even what week it was. In fact, a sizable minority, including Mr. Nouvelle, seemed to have given up on this particular real world and slipped off to someplace where, as yet, I could not follow even in my imagination.

Finally, in early winter Mr. Nouvelle offered me a glimpse of his private world. He materialized before me just outside the dayroom and quietly, intensely told me that he remembered me from long ago.

"I, ahh, . . . watch you now all the time," he said, twisting his hands nervously, "and I think that perhaps—maybe a long time ago—I think that I was the husband dinosaur and you were the wife dinosaur." He went on to tell me that he was a Nicodemosaurus and I a Tracodamosaurus and that as such we had privileges not shared by others on the ward. If I could arrange to get him a day pass, for example, he would drive me around the neighboring town of Hillsdale in a limousine, escorted by a dozen motorcycles, he added, noting my hesitation. Escorted by fleets of cars. Accompanied by bulldozers. And in my mind's eye I tried adding bulldozers to a wilder, leafier landscape where hazel-eyed dinosaurs roamed in search of cigarette butts and half-empty cans of Coca-Cola.

"But, ahh . . . , Miss Baur," he called me back. "I could arrange to go by myself, but, ahh . . . , that's no good. You need to share such an experience for it to, ahh . . . Do you see?"

"Yes," I answered, pulling myself back from an imaginary Cretaceous. "Yes indeed," and I nodded, encouraging the familiar idea of sharing. And suddenly we were talking about sex, or rather he was talking, but I, not having made the transition, momentarily maintained the companionable stance of the previous conversation.

"Of course, I try not to touch myself and, uhh, keep chaste," he was saying, the words now tumbling over themselves. "But if I were with a woman now. If I were touched, I would probably just go—"And he snapped his right forearm rigid, bent at the elbow.

A dozen ways to flee flashed across my mind.

"Are you leaving me now?" asked Mr. Nouvelle, reading my thoughts as persons with near-intolerable levels of sensitivity are often able to do.

"Yes," I answered.

"But you aren't leaving me forever . . . yet." And he smiled a quizzical smile and held me a moment more with magnified eyes.

That was my introduction to Mr. Nouvelle. This small, soft-spoken man was indeed creating entire cosmologies in his head, and, although he was clearly delusional, he had masterfully outmaneuvered each of my attempts to keep the conversation running along a somewhat ordinary path.

As I disentangled myself from his ideas, he floated back to the far corner of the dayroom and knelt before one of the heavy brown chairs that sat in two straight rows in front of the television set. One of the aides had already told me that Mr. Nouvelle performed unnatural acts on invisible men, but from where I stood I could not tell whether the Nicodemosaurus was bobbing up and down or simply praying. I watched for a moment or two and wondered what was going on. Perhaps if I got to know him . . .

Abruptly, I set off down the corridor in search of the ward psychologist to see if I could become Mr. Nouvelle's case manager and therapist. Two days later the Dinosaur Man and I began meeting several times a week.

Initially, Mr. Nouvelle and I met in a small room across from the nurses' station. We sat on opposite sides of a long Formica table around which crowded a dozen mismatched chairs. From where I sat, I could see a broken exercycle, a full-length mirror, and a single window that looked out on a square of wintry sky. From where he sat, he could see anything he wanted, including scenes that, although not entirely clear, made me squirm.

Our early meetings were totally confusing. He was a Venetian policeman, the Inspector General, my father, or even me, and in turn I was mother, wife, son, daughter, duck egg, and dinosaur. All of us were connected by events we could not remember, and none of us knew who we would turn into from minute to minute. Bedrock was quicksand, walls were pits, yes meant no, and every word we used slid out from under its usual meaning and hustled us toward sex or violence.

"N. cherished yesward," Mr. Nouvelle wrote on the first page of a blank book that I gave him to keep as a diary.

"Yesward? The yes word?" I queried.

"Like the Negro girls," he explained, leaning toward me as far as he could across the table and fixing me with an intense stare. "When they say 'Noooooo,' that means they like it a lot."

"Did you ever meet a Negro girl?" I asked quickly, hoping to reel him back toward reality.

"Noooooo," he said again, still staring, imploring. "When a woman has too much Mother, which is not good for a grown man, she mustn't pull out her words like 'Ooooooo, Maurice, come onnnn.' So I punched her in the head and on the floor. I beat her head on the floor, and she lay there curled up like a baby. 'Are you all right?' 'Noooooo.' But I did what was right."

"Mr. Nouvelle," I answered, after watching him silently relive the rest of an incident which, according to his record, had indeed occurred, "Mr. Nouvelle, do not hit me. Do you understand?"

"I frightened you, didn't I?"

And so the conversations went—many utterly incomprehensible, others making more and more sense as I learned his language. At first he was loathe to tell me what special terms like *indooblecate* or *Hannah Barra* meant, and I was forced to extricate them from dense forests of fantasies. Hannah Barra, for example, was not a woman as I first imagined nor, apparently, an abbreviated reference to Hanna-Barbera, the syndicate that produced television's dinosaur clan "The Flintstones." Instead, it was a place, similar to a "habi-tat," where every day Mr. Nouvelle met with each of his six occidental wives. One of these women crawled around on all fours and thus reminded Mr. Nouvelle of a goat. Another was a chipmunk who forced him into the role of amorous woodchuck. Others were ordinary women. He insisted that the goat-woman lived in a Hannah Barra in Canada, where I suspected he had visited with his father, and the chipmunk lived on the blueberry barrens. Months passed before I discovered that the goat-wife was a gym teacher at the hospital who did indeed get down on her hands and knees, and the chipmunk-wife was a round-cheeked young woman who assisted in one of the testing laboratories. I guessed that his other wives were connected to real women too, but all seemed so far removed from their original characters and settings that I was not sure if Mr. Nouvelle could ever move them back in his mind from fantasies toward ordinary memories.

Indooblecate was harder to track down, but eventually I realized that it referred to the terrible "fogs-on-my-mind" that "ruined" him without warning. One minute Mr. Nouvelle felt himself to be a sophisticated man, a "doctoreate" at a university preparing his lecture or God the Father gathering goodness for the

Mass; in the next instant he was indooblecated and thus left alone, in pain and utterly impotent.

"I *told* them I was the son who never sucked dick," he wailed. "I promised not to eat anything until my eyes were fixed. I gave the sign"—and here he kissed the ends of his fingers from little finger to thumb and back again—"but still they cut into my brain and took it out by the pailful. When are they going to *fix* me and send me home to my wives?"

Moments like these blew across Mr. Nouvelle's mind like cloud shadows across the uncut fields behind the hospital, and I wondered if I were observing the reactions of a person so sensitive to frustration that the slightest setback threw him into a panic or if I were watching the uncontrollable short-circuiting of a disordered brain. In other words, were his fits of gloom and panic connected to childhood trauma? Or more simply and hopelessly to an imbalance of chemical messengers in his brain that turned the nod of a head and the shimmer of Jell-O on his lunch tray into nameless horrors?

For a time now I had been given tantalizing glimpses of Mr. Nouvelle's early years. He told me that his father, Jesus-Peter-and-Paul, was no good because he couldn't lift any of his sons, and he told me that for the first two years of his life he slept in a crib with his two sisters. He loved seeing them with their nightdresses pulled up high on their little bodies and was sad when his mother moved him into the boys' room when he threatened to poke out his sisters' eyes. He said, moreover, that he could remember a photograph of himself as a very young child dressed in stockings and a tunic and posed with his dearest friends, the saints and angels.

Well, so much for all that information, I thought.

"What are the names of your brothers and sisters?" I asked on several occasions, and each time Mr. Nouvelle gave me eight or nine names, and each time they were different. The only consistent information was that his father was named Jesus-Peter-and-Paul (which I doubted) and that one or two of the names always had a French-Canadian flavor. At first I thought he had forgotten the names of his family, perhaps because of all the electric shock treatments and medications he had received, but gradually it occurred to me that he was hoarding the names like a treasure. This reluctance to reveal anything about himself functioned, as did his lurid sexual fantasies, to hold people at arm's length. The stronger he came on, it seemed, the less he really told me about himself.

This reluctance to reveal himself did not hold true of his dinosaur identity, however, and soon I learned a great deal about the living habits of these enormous beasts. On average, dinosaurs lived for 100 million years, and each ordinary day seemed to them like "days within days and years within years." Especially on winter afternoons when the snow swirled between the steep-roofed hospital buildings and the dinosaurs drifted among them like enormous shadows, time stood still, frozen and unpromising. "Will it ever be spring for me?" the dinosaurs asked then, and the mother dinosaur in each family told the six big wife dinosaurs and the one smaller husband dinosaur about the old days, when the grass was high and green and the farmers put out piles of pumpkins for them to eat. There were Coke machines in the meadows then, and around them were scattered all the cigarette butts anyone could want.

Over the next several months, as winter locked Mountain Valley into a glittering costume of snow, I became a part of this family. My mother, Beatrice, was one of Mr. Nouvelle's dinosaur-wives. I was his daughter, a relationship he finally settled on because, he told me, I knew so little.

One afternoon, as Mr. Nouvelle sat in the dayroom smoking a pipe with a curious pitted bowl, which he insisted came from the leg of an octopus, I addressed him in French. I asked how he had spent the day. A long pause ensued, and, just as I began to repeat the question in English, he interrupted me—in French. I was astonished.

"How did you learn French?" I asked when he fell silent.

"My mother spoke it. I can remember playing with cars on the kitchen floor while my mother and a friend had coffee and chatted in French."

"And what was your mother's name?" I asked, reverting to French in the hope of continuing to outflank his delusions.

21

"Indian."

"She was Indian."

"Partly, but the nuns called her Agnes Theresa Marie."

"And your father's name?" I went on, expecting to run up against Jesus.

"French. Pierre-Paul."

Over the next several weeks Mr. Nouvelle allowed me to exhume portions of his childhood that had been buried under mountainous piles of delusions. (I was later able to confirm this information through one of his brothers.) Mr. Nouvelle was born in a small logging town not far from the Canadian border, the youngest of nine children, and came into the world to replace a daughter born barely a year earlier, who had died of whooping cough. Her name was Claudine, and the family called Maurice by his middle name, Claude. Times were hard for the family in those years. His father was apparently drinking to dull the pain of an old back injury, and his mother, still mourning the death of her baby, was sad and very, very tired. The care of Maurice fell to his four older sisters, and it was they who dressed him in frocks like a girl or a doll and pushed him around in a big wicker baby carriage.

When Maurice was six, he began attending a parochial school where the nuns spoke French as well as English. He quickly got the reputation of being a bright boy, and later, when his IQ was tested, he was indeed found to be of superior intelligence. About third grade, however, his troubles began to surface. He took to masturbating three or four times a day on the living-room couch, especially when his father, who could rarely work now because of his back, went off to Canada to stay with his brothers.

"Now you will have to treat me like the Father," he remembered saying. Maurice also began to join in the games of his older brother, such as "dick flicking" in the woods behind the school, but he was always the youngest and smallest, and something of his early years as a "girl" led the older boys to taunt him.

There were happy memories as well—trips to his uncle's sugar maple farm, picking beans with his father, and running off to the local parish to help Father Victor Bisette with the rabbits and chickens. "I had a craving to hold chickens in my hands and kiss their wattles," he remembered. " 'Piiiti-piti-piti-piti.' I called them in from under the pear trees just like Father Bisette."

There was a point, however, beyond which Mr. Nouvelle would not pass in his reminiscing. He told me of his attempt to be an acolyte and of the confusing yearnings that this experience had provoked. He took me through "a clear time" in high school when he had belonged to the Future Farmers of America and had worn his blue jacket with the tractor emblem on it to school. He even told me of his first year at the logging camp where he had gone to work when his mother could no longer afford to feed him. But further he would not go in either French or English, and why or how he was first hospitalized remained a mystery.

Nor was speaking French quite the circumvention that I had hoped it would be. Sometimes he acted as if he didn't understand the language at all, and even when he did his delusions increasingly overran this forgotten island of innocent memories. French neologisms moved into his English vocabulary, and, when he spoke of being "indooblecated," for example, he added *désutrit,* which I took to be an aberration of the French word for "destroyed." His delusions concerning sex, greatness, and persecution also flowed into his French, and he was soon able to discuss "being queered" or squeezing zucchini in either language.

But no matter what the mixture of languages was on any given day, certain subjects were off-limits. If I questioned him too closely, he would stop abruptly and frown, as if finding himself in a disagreeable place.

"I don't think I like you anymore," he would say. "I think the Father just took all the goodness out of me for Communion tomorrow."

"Have *I* taken something out of you?" I asked. "Do I know too much about you now?"

Mr. Nouvelle's answer was incomprehensible. However, he repeated "taking away" several times, and, as was his custom when agitated, he took an imaginary dick from his pocket and began sucking on it. Clearly this curious man desired to be understood, and just as clearly the giving away of his secrets and rediscovery of his past felt extremely dangerous to him.

Even with pieces missing, an outline of Mr. Nouvelle's life made it easier for me to understand his convoluted language and baroque delusions, both of which seemed tensely stretched between sex and Catholicism. Before knowing he had been active in the Future Farmers of America, for example, I had not understood why duck eggs and chicken wattles played such a large part in his sexual fantasies and why fruits and vegetables were so frequently substituted for those parts of a woman's anatomy that he loved to linger over in his mind. These luscious remnants of a rural upbringing were an especially important part of his lovemaking "under sodium" with the "invisible ladies." "Under sodium" apparently referred to a time when he had been given Sodium Amytal to help him sleep. Sexual fantasies had visited him in his dreams then, and so impressed was he by their vividness that he had learned to evoke them each night when he went to bed. Since these delights were imposed upon him by a drug—or even the memory of a drug—he could not be blamed for either having them or enjoying them. And enjoy them he did.

About eleven every evening, the patients on 9-2-D changed into their pajamas and, after a last cigarette call, retired to the dormitories. These were big, airy rooms in which six-foot-high partitions marked off areas about eight feet square. In each of these areas was a bed, a bureau, and an armoire. There were no doors.

The dormitories were not peaceful at night. Restless patients were up and down incessantly. Others wet their beds and had to be showered and changed. Still others called out in their dreams or moaned as they masturbated. The moaning so disturbed one patient that he threatened to stab the sinners in their sleep with his ballpoint pen. In spite of such distractions, which, in actual fact, did not lead to harm, Mr. Nouvelle managed to believe that the nightly safety check made around 2:00 A.M. was a "dick inspection," and that this was the signal for the invisible ladies to come into his bed. Occidental beauties they were—although he never described them to me in detail—and like a warm breeze in summer or the tepid stream of water that a black woman pours down a man's pants, they flowed along the tiled corridors of 9-2-D, slipped under the closed door of the dorm, and sinuously wafted over and around the partitions that divided the patients' "rooms." Insinuating themselves like slender fingers under his green hospital blanket, the invisible ladies trembled down the length of Mr. Nouvelle's body, and he became aroused. So did the women, he explained, and the cantaloupes between their legs ran with the same fragrant juice he had tasted in the hot fields behind his boyhood home. Warm milk began to gather in the pit of his stomach.

There followed nightly orgies of incredible proportions, the descriptions of which sounded like the rich interleafing of a pornographic novel and a poultry breeder's manual. Sweet milk ran from wombs and penises, a son sucked his mother's zucchini, and duck eggs moved throughout the male and female anatomy as easily as one draws a breath. Soon the invisible ladies moaned in ecstasy, as Mr. Nouvelle drove his thirty-eight good dicks into their cantaloupes and streams of green beans poured from the women's fingers and out their ears. But as soon as the connection was made, it was annulled. Amid protestations of blamelessness, the exhausted Mr. Nouvelle assured the Father that he was still an untouched virgin. The Father Himself had sent these ladies, he told me, and even though they had had intercourse, the experience did not count. And indeed it did not.

At first, I believed that the relationship between Mr. Nouvelle's intense desire for fornication and his equally intense need of God's protection was one of fairly straightforward conflict. Because sex was a sin and would lead to damnation, Mr. Nouvelle had worked out a way of passively enduring sexual delights while remaining blameless and, alas, uncomforted. As I learned more, however, it began to appear that his yearning for a perfect and everlasting union with God actually fueled his desire for women and vice versa. The Father needed to give Mr. Nouvelle invisible ladies to prove both His power and His compassion, and the ladies could not have unleashed their full and ferocious passion on Mr. Nouvelle unless God were at hand to temper their assault on his emotions. Of course, there was also an out-and-out conflict between loving and sinning, connecting and remaining alone, just as earlier in his life he had felt "caught betwixt" loving his mother or father, his sisters or brothers, and his own femaleness or maleness.

These not uncommon conflicts were complicated in Mr. Nouvelle's case by the different levels on which he could make love. On each of his three levels he struck a different balance between connectedness and isolation, and on all levels both these states had dangers and delights.

With the invisible ladies—whether in his bed at night or in the Hannah Barras he constructed for his wives—lovemaking was largely without substance and without risk. They were not, as he termed it, "really real." On the other hand, making love to the "real women who stand in front of me" was more satisfactory, except that it involved the possibility of rejection and took a little more explaining to God. The first of these pitfalls Mr. Nouvelle tried to avoid by hiding his intentions, in fact by hiding the entire act from his partners, and the second he skirted by letting the Father have the final say on whether or not "it" happened.

Every female in the hospital, from age fifteen to sixty, from patient to psychiatrist, was Mr. Nouvelle's unknowing partner. Upon spotting a woman, Mr. Nouvelle would glide up to within about two feet of her and stare intently at her nose or breasts. Then, without warning, "it" might happen. Her clothes would vaporize, she'd give a nervous little laugh (or better still, touch her nose), and her cantaloupe would open. It was over in a second, although sometimes Mr. Nouvelle could extend the pleasure by saying a magic word.

"Nosy-weezy?" he would ask as he stepped away.

"Uh . . . , sure, Mr. Nouvelle," a nurse or an aide might say, and Mr. Nouvelle, now assured that she had felt "it" too, felt good for hours. If, on the other hand, the woman drew back and frowned, then her clothes stayed on and her face began to rot in a disgusting way. This meant that God had allowed her to be taken over by Mr. Nouvelle's enemies, and those faceless forces were ever on the lookout for ways of denying him pleasure. The woman herself had "gone haggy" on him, and when this happened Mr. Nouvelle felt so frustrated and upset that he would not eat for the rest of the day.

The highest level of lovemaking was "flesh on flesh," and I was relieved to learn that God the Father would consider this a mortal sin. "You can't be the one I do it with flesh on flesh," he explained. "It won't be very good for me because I haven't been indoctrinated."

Lovemaking on each of the three levels also occurred with men, although it seemed to me that Mr. Nouvelle's desultory homosexuality was prompted more by the easy availability of men than by a real preference for them. I had watched Mr. Nouvelle take the arms of an empty wooden armchair in his hands, kneel before it, and bob silently up and down, and I had seen him play around with a man known as the Extortionist. The two would bump into each other or poke halfheartedly at each other's private parts. Mr. Nouvelle told me that once he gave a patient a dollar to follow him into the basement of Building 2 and there let him reach into his pants. Because he found no "dick," but "only a small zucchini," he knew he had chosen a man who was really a woman.

Regardless of whether a man or a woman was the object of the Dinosaur Man's desire, his outrageous methods of seduction guaranteed that he would be rejected or left unsatisfied. Recalling his dramatic masturbations on the living-room couch, I guessed that this push-and-pull technique of simultaneously attracting and repelling affection had been used for a long time. It kept an early message fresh in Mr. Nouvelle's mind, namely, "you will be punished if you ask for love." But what if a really real person accepted his verbal advances? What would this do to his delicately balanced system of securities?

As winter moved into what, for most people, would be spring, I began to see that my presence was having an effect on Mr. Nouvelle's imaginary comforts. He had apparently decided that although befriending me entailed the great and familiar dangers of rejection, abandonment, and enslavement, he could risk the connection if we merged and became identical. Thus he expressed an intense desire to be exactly like me. No matter how I took my coffee, he took his the same way, and no matter how many cookies I ate, he ate exactly the same number. He refused to express any differences of opinion, and he insisted that as "capital T-true father and daughter" we had been born on the same day. Nevertheless, he could not help feeling uneasy. Something peculiar was happening to his wives.

"Am I going to be able to leave you and go on with my other lives?" he once asked. Or again, quite possibly saying the reverse of what he meant, "My wives aren't acting like good wives. They say I don't satisfy them."

As the snow melted and widening pools of brown lawn spread out around each building, it became apparent that Mr. Nouvelle's wives were leaving him, and in a particularly tormenting way. One afternoon, for example, we set out in search of pussy willows. As we left Building 9, a car drove into the visitors' parking lot, and two middle-aged women got out. With a happy start of recognition, Mr. Nouvelle headed straight for the taller of the two women with love on his mind. Just as abruptly, he reversed himself and slouched dejectedly back to me.

"Who was that?" I asked.

"She did it again," he moaned. "That was Betsy, but as soon as she saw me she turned into a stranger."

Mr. Nouvelle went on to explain that this taunting form of rejection was occurring frequently now. He would spot one of his wives, move toward her, and be cut off from his pleasure by a sudden transmogrification. Of course, it did not occur to Mr. Nouvelle that either his own memory of Betsy was unraveling—as his picture of me would undoubtedly decompose when I left Mountain Valley—or his ability to delude himself and thereby change what *is* into what *could be* was losing its power. Those were my explanations. His were that his wives were angry at him for spending so much time with me or that I, being a killjoy of the worst sort, was ordering them to stay away. In either case, he understood that my presence worked against his magical pleasures and that therapy had a decidedly dark side.

I too was concerned with his loss of comfort. Although gratified to see Mr. Nouvelle's nearly forty-year-old system of delusions begin to soften and change, I was distressed to realize that Betsy, the goat-wife, and others were not fading into some kind of benevolent, personal legend. They were not becoming dinosaurs, for example, nor were their deeds and characters being grafted onto the memory of a beloved grandmother or a good doctor. Instead, it seemed that whatever small comforts the gym teacher or the ward psychiatrist had given Mr. Nouvelle (and which he had then transformed and exaggerated in his mind) were simply being lost along with his delusions. What a price to pay for a little sanity, I thought, and wondered what would become of his memory of me and of my affection for him when I was gone.

There was a brighter side to these changes, of course, and if my presence was diluting the authenticity of Mr. Nouvelle's six wives, it was also enhancing his own in small ways. For one thing, he was spending more time as "plain Mr. Nouvelle"; for another, he was able to switch in and out of his delusional world with greater ease; and for a third, he was receiving somewhat more respect on the ward from both patients and staff. These changes were subtle. For example, one of his standard fantasies—roaming through the nurses' locker room as an invisible spirit—grew flexible enough first to permit me to join him on these expeditions and then to be voluntarily turned off in favor of remaining in my world.

"Well, I don't need invisible nurses," he would say smoothly when I declined to accompany him into fantasyland. "I have you."

On other occasions, when his imagination would suddenly ricochet off a provocative word and send him careening down a chasm of bizarre associations, he found he could pull himself back with my help. In fact, one of the most effective ways to recall him was to go a little cuckoo myself. Thus, when he went off on a tangent about "St. Barn-a-bus . . . Barn O'Busse . . . Barna . . . Barna," I interrupted with something to the effect that every farmer needs a mobile shelter for cows called a Barn-on-a-bus.

"Miss Baur," said Mr. Nouvelle, snapping instantly back to the present, "how am I going to teach you anything if you insist on being so silly?"

Even with a nascent ability to disembark from his own runaway trains of thought, Mr. Nouvelle still believed that his only hope of safety lay in merging with me, and this he found increasingly hard to do. He continued to construct a joint past which linked us like twins, he tried literally to dive into my stomach one morning during Mass, and he continually attempted to pull me into his world. But none of these tactics carried him closer to the promised land of total and unqualified love. Nothing satisfied the old Nicodemosaurus, who, with increasing frustration, seemed to ask, "How can a man be born when he is old? Can he enter a second time into his mother's womb and be born?"

One afternoon Mr. Nouvelle gave me $100,000 in invisible money and was annoyed I would not give him a dollar bill in exchange. He then insisted women had "d-i-c-s" and was annoyed that I would not agree to that either. And he listened to his brother Terry's voice and couldn't believe that I could not hear it also. Finally retreating to a topic that might restore our sense of unity, he asked if I had seen my mother lately. "No," I replied, not spotting the danger in time, "she lives far from here."

Months of fear and frustration burst to the surface.

"That's not possible!" he shouted, his face flushing and his pupils contracting to pinholes. "My dinosaur wife lives behind Building 9. If you are my daughter, she must be your mother!"

Both alarmed and betrayed—how dare this patient use logic and delusion at the same time—I scrambled to regain control of the conversation. "Does it frighten you to feel separate from me?" I asked.

"No!" he roared, getting to his feet. "No, I am not frightening, but I need your goodness. They've taken all mine out and left me betwixt. *Betwixt! Indooblecated! Désutrit!*" Mr. Nouvelle slammed back into his seat, vomiting a geyser of incomprehensible anger. He banged his head on the table. He clawed at the crown-of-thorn scabs he kept open on his forehead. He held on to the edge of the table and shook. Abruptly he relaxed, face down on the table.

"What . . . am . . . I . . . supposed . . . to . . . do?" he finally asked, rising slowly to his feet, his voice anguished. "What do I have to do? Rape you? Attack you? Just to get you into my arms? You have taken me over, but you won't give me what I have to have. I will not meet with you anymore."

And with that Mr. Nouvelle walked calmly and deliberately out of the room.

Alone in the meeting room in the late afternoon, I stared at the shadow of the exercycle that climbed up and over the bulletin board on the inside wall. I felt terrible. Great and familiar dangers, indeed, I thought to myself. And had I imagined myself immune from the hurt of losing someone I cared for? I saw myself then as the latest in a straggling line of people from whom Mr. Nouvelle had sought love and understanding. When he was born, his parents were so overwhelmed with raising a huge family in a hard time that they simply did not have those gifts to give, and as he grew and was beset by more than his natural share of uncertainty and confusion, no one came into his life equipped to handle his exorbitant demands.

"Just stop it, Claude," he remembered one of the nuns saying to him. "Talk normal or we aren't going to talk at all."

So now it was my turn to stand up against this old and unsolvable problem. Would I too meet his demands with a demand of my own—just stop it, and be normal? Would I drift away or stay but stop trying? What would it take, I wondered, to be the first person to step out of that long line of expectations, to be the first not to repeat "You will be punished if you ask for love."

Over the next month, as the days lengthened and the trees along the drive leafed out, Mr. Nouvelle and I embarked upon a new kind of relationship. Although still preoccupied with sex, he increasingly treated me as "steady backer" and a "pal."

"You know," he once told me in a whisper so that no one else would catch on, "a man needs a steady pal, just one steady pal for life."

So we became pals. He helped me make signs for the ward bulletin board. I showed him how to fix a zipper. He saved pictures for me of ladies' underwear. I gave him magazines. Together we started a vegetable garden. We even began to disagree, as chums sometimes will, and he would not let me weed the garden until all the lettuce and bean seedlings had come up, for fear I would disturb them.

"But the seedlings will come up between the stakes," I argued. "Everything else is a weed."

"How do *you* know where those seeds travel when they're underground?" he asked with a superior air, and from then on took full command of the gardening.

Our small plot, tucked behind an abandoned greenhouse and flanked by the fields in the back of the hospital, became a happy place for Mr. Nouvelle. Perhaps because it reminded him of his family's garden or his association with the Future Farmers of America, it made it easier for him to remember some of the happier times of his life. One afternoon he decided that he, alone, would transplant some seedlings. I was to watch and carry water. From the shade of a small pear tree whose drops were already attracting yellow jackets as the summer wore on, I watched Mr. Nouvelle transplant marigolds with a plastic spoon. For a long time he was silent, and I wondered what part of his past or what portion of his imaginary world he was living in. Then he began to sing what sounded like an old French lullaby.

Mr. Nouvelle sang to his seedlings as he tucked them into the ground, and I remembered a time, years before, when I had walked through what seemed like a trackless stretch of underbrush and had come upon the faint signs of an old roadway. I had followed that trail, more by feeling than seeing, and, as I watched Mr. Nouvelle digging in the dirt with his spoon, I felt again the elation of coming upon an old marker that connected me to the past, to a person, to the business of living. It filled me with joy to watch Mr. Nouvelle being, at least for these few minutes, a happy and contented man.

When the transplanting was finished, we washed our hands

under a spigot and started back by way of a farm pond. Like a pair of sleepwalkers we drifted down the fields, Mr. Nouvelle still dreaming of an earlier time, I turning to sad thoughts of saying good-bye. Although I had not yet told Mr. Nouvelle, our time together was drawing to a close. When the beans we had just cultivated were harvested, my job would end on 9-2-D.

"The world is a different place for me," said Mr. Nouvelle, breaking into my thoughts.

"How long has that been so?"

"Always."

"Since you left home and went to work?" I asked, still curious to know more about that period of his life.

"Yes . . . , since my eyes went bad and I began having those stoppages of the murdered mind."

As we approached the pond, a school of fingerlings darted into the shallows, and abruptly, matter-of-factly, Mr. Nouvelle recounted the story of his first hospitalization—how he believed the men at the logging camp thought he was queer, how they had sent messages to him through the cosmic whine of the screeching saws, and how at last he'd been carried off the job with crazy sounds of wheezing and jeering in his ears. Sometime later he had been taken to a hospital, and there he was questioned, medicated, and given shock treatments that "walk the thoughts right out of your mind." Finally he was taken home and there met by a family who "looked at me like an animal."

"That was *not* a good time," he said sadly, and, as had happened before, Mr. Nouvelle began to cry.

During the next several days Mr. Nouvelle gave me the uncanny impression that he knew I was going to announce my departure.

"Summer could end at any moment," he would say cryptically, as we shaded our lettuce against the hot July sun. Or "my sisters told me they'd visit me on my birthday, but when I woke up my birthday had passed. I never saw them again." But above all Mr. Nouvelle seemed intent on telling me how much he wanted a taste of ordinary life, just a decade or so of perfect bliss surrounded by adoring women who would cook for him without their clothes on. These stories got all mixed up with God. Sometimes Mr. Nouvelle himself was God, and other times the Father took His favorite son in His hands and carried him to the vine-covered cottage where all that cooking went on. The theme that was constant throughout was Mr. Nouvelle's desperate yearning for a perfect and everlasting union.

One afternoon, as we sat in the deep shade of a maple, Mr. Nouvelle made a heroic attempt to blast himself into an orbit of heavenly peace. It was one of the strangest performances I have ever seen, and to this day I can only guess at what was going on. For half an hour Mr. Nouvelle's memory and imagination seemed engaged in a private transaction of considerable urgency. They rattled on about disappearing days, invisible beans, and other of their private quarrels, and gradually I noticed that passages from the Bible were being invoked, perhaps for emphasis. At first there were only a few words—"Thy will be done"—then longer and longer phrases were added. To my amazement, long selections came pouring out with increasing speed.

"Jesus said unto her, 'I am the resurrection and the life: he that believeth in me, though he were dead, yet shall he live.'

"I am the man that hath seen affliction," he recited, going faster still. "He hath led me, and brought me into darkness, but not into light. . . . My flesh and my skin hath he made old; He hath broken my bones. . . . He hath set me in dark places, as they that be dead."

Back and forth careened Mr. Nouvelle, now dying, now being reborn. Tears began to roll down the old Nicodemosaurus's face, but his pace did not slow. He was thrashing his way toward heaven.

"Except a man be born again, he cannot see the kingdom of God. And Nicodemus saith unto him, 'How can a man be born when he is old? Can he enter a second time . . . ?' Tell me! Tell me! Can he?"

Was I watching a miracle or seeing a man drown? I burst into tears.

34

Mr. Nouvelle stopped his recitation and tenderly took my hands in his.

"I made you sad?" he asked in surprise. "Or are you too happy? Or are you happy and sad at the same time?" I nodded, tears streaming down my face. I had no reply.

Nor did Mr. Nouvelle have a reply when I told him the next day that I was leaving 9-2-D and would no longer be meeting with him. We had a month of gardening left. For nearly a week Mr. Nouvelle ignored this news and then with unbearable energy called back all the magic he had ever used to endure thirty-seven years of chaos and loneliness. He went on a hunger strike and lost 15 pounds. He stuffed his jacket pockets with invisible dicks and sucked on them incessantly. He made the sign by kissing his fingers not once but three times, and he increased his number of wives to a thousand and then to a hundred thousand. He even tried to back up his magic with logic. Would I stay if he spoke French? If he took me to Mass? Was I tired of him? Had I expected him to marry me?

One afternoon, Mr. Nouvelle was sent back to the ward from occupational therapy, where he had been coloring owls in a coloring book. He had begun sticking his fingers down his throat in an attempt to remove a woman who was lodged there, and now, still coughing and gagging, he was as upset as I'd ever seen him. We sat in the old meeting room for a few minutes, but he would not speak. Abruptly he began to weep. Tears rolled down his thin face, and his shoulders began to shake. Clenching his fists and locking his jaw, he arched backward in his chair and then, without warning, threw his head down on the table. I could hear his glasses crack. He had told me earlier that at unpredictable times he "died in agony," and I surmised that I was witnessing one of these times. When the goodness in himself and the world drained completely away, he had said, it felt like being eaten alive by rats. He could hear his own bones break over and over again, and sometimes his face would rot and slough off. This time the pain seemed to come from being abandoned.

"Are they dead forever?" he asked between sobs. "The Father and the good images? Will I never have them again?"

Minutes passed as Mr. Nouvelle threw himself again and again against the inescapable hurt of parting and against the unjustifiable confusion that permeated every minute of his life.

"I am afraid," he finally said, raising his head from the table. "I am afraid everything will be over and I won't have had anything. Does a dinosaur, I mean a dinosaur's daughter, understand that?"

The last two weeks with the Dinosaur Man were terrible. He was upset and delusional, and there were no reprieves. During our last meeting he caught sight of a new patient, a man of about twenty-five. He stared across the hall at him and poured into that stare the same intense question and promise that he'd held in his eyes when he first looked at me, and before me at his six wives, at a hundred nurses, and at all the women in the world.

"Miss Baur," he asked, still staring at the patient, "am I obliged to stay with you the whole hour?"

"No, Mr. Nouvelle."

"I see Tommy Hammond over there with a bag in his hand," he continued, swaying toward the young man. "He may be my dinosaur son, and I think he has something for me."

And thus we said good-bye as the million-year cycle of betrayal and enchantment began again, and I did not think I would ever know whether or not the Dinosaur Man could carry in his heart the memory that for a day within a day and a year within a year someone had cared for him a great deal.

Approximately one year later, I had occasion to revisit 9-2-D. In the meantime I had heard that Mr. Nouvelle was behaving as he always had. He continued to stare, to talk incomprehensibly about sex, and to forage for Coke cans and cigarette butts. As I unlocked the ward's heavy wooden door, I recalled the questions I had asked when I first met Mr. Nouvelle. Had I been watching a man wounded in childhood? Or struggling against a disordered brain? I was inclined to answer yes to both questions now. The tapestry of sexual delusions that he had woven in the course of nearly forty years was so disquieting to everyone that it protected him from making meaningful contact with "real" people who, he had learned earlier, were confusing and hurtful. Mr. Nouvelle's delusions also seemed to express his need to compensate for the constant short-circuiting of a disordered brain—a brain so unable to keep time or memories or facts in order that it was always dealing with fractured experience. Delusions were his imaginative explanations for chaos.

I had not known enough when I first arrived at Mountain Valley to ask a third question, namely, did Mr. Nouvelle's bizarre behavior also serve to sustain the belief that he was a lovable person and a valuable member of a community in a place where he was not, in fact, deeply loved or valued? The answer to that question also appeared to be yes. It no longer seemed strange to me that Mr. Nouvelle was not anxious to give up his delusions. In fact, as I walked down the familiar pink-tiled corridor, I thought to myself that any person who wanted to stay alive in a situation where there was no hope for love or health or meaningful work would have to be crazy to admit to himself that his dreams of love, health, and work were only fantasies.

As I stood before the ward bulletin board copying a list of names, up floated Mr. Nouvelle, frowning deeply.

"You have been here all this time," he said accusingly. "You just didn't want my eyes to see you."

Before I could reply, he turned his back on me and crouched before a warped metal mirror that reflected only freaks.

"My mind has been irrelevant since you left," he continued in confusion. "I forgot you. I forgot everything you said to me."

"Everything?" I queried as I prepared to leave.

"Everything," he answered.

Suddenly the old Dinosaur Man himself stood up and stared intently at me through dust-speckled glasses. He smiled his quizzical smile and held me a moment more with his magnified eyes.

"Everything," he repeated, "except the words of love."

The Reconstruction of
Dr. Sweetheart

Flying through the memories of several patients on 9-2-D are the glorious afterimages of the fantastic Dr. Sweetheart. He flew when other doctors walked. He cured while others sat around. He prescribed naked women as well as pills, and, best of all, he continued to live on the roof of Building 2, where he spied benignly on his favorite patients through a long glass. I first met the doctor's arresting name on a patient's chart: then I encountered the memories themselves.

I was sitting in a meeting room at Mountain Valley Hospital with Dallas Grey, a small, elusive patient, and I asked him to tell me what helped the most. Usually vague to the point of utter incoherence, Mr. Grey answered decisively, "Dr. Sweetheart."

"Dr. Sweetheart," he continued after a long pause, "took me like a father and a son. He promised me a nude woman. 'But you have to get her yourself, Dallas.' You see, if I got well, he would make it work."

I knew from previous conversations that *it* had not always

worked and that this uncertainty, among dozens of others, made Mr. Grey apprehensive of women.

But gradually, over a period of time that Mr. Grey felt like calling "two years or seven or six," he improved, and one day his favorite nurse, Pookie Hauptmann, supposedly said, "Dallas, go for it."

"So I walked out into the snow, and sure enough I found a woman and we went together for two years and had intercourse. Well, we tried, and it ranged from good to extraordinary. Dr. Sweetheart said he'd check her 'V' out for VD if she agrees to it and she did. So I had a free mind for a while with no mind reading or voices and now it's over and he has to start over and over."

"And where is Dr. Sweetheart now?" I asked, wondering why I had not encountered this charismatic doctor.

"Flying down the corridors like Superman," answered Mr. Grey, with his broad, buck-toothed grin. "Flying with a cape."

That was my initial introduction to Dr. Sweetheart, and some subtle shift in Mr. Grey's demeanor as he talked of his hero made me suspect that some of what I'd learned was true. Thus I set out to ask everyone I encountered, "Who was this Dr. Sweetheart?"

It did not take me long to learn that Franklin Leroy Sweetheart was a black physician from Chicago who had indeed worked at Mountain Valley Hospital. Apparently he had graduated from a no-name medical school, as the ward psychiatrist put it, and had spent the first fifteen or twenty years of his career in the army. There he had earnestly contemplated the statement "the army travels on its feet" and interpreted it to mean that healthy feet are essential for healthy living. Thus he arrived at Mountain Valley with pedicure instruments protruding from the pocket of his white coat and a somewhat quixotic determination to alleviate whatever discomforts his skills could address.

"Dr. Sweetheart was a handsome man," said Mr. Grey one afternoon, as I walked him to the greenhouse to learn if he had really been fired from his hospital job for threatening to kill the president of the United States. "He was a little tall . . . like me, and he had a lot more black hair."

"A little tall?" I asked, looking at Dallas Grey, who might have been five foot six in shoes.

"Oh yes, when he walked me around the hospital and told me about all the things that happened. When he prepared the medicines. He kept me occupied."

"And how old was he?"

"Thirty-three," replied Mr. Grey, giving me his own age.

"Do you still see him?" I asked, picturing to myself a handsome black doctor in a white coat striding down the corridors with tiny Dallas Grey jogging silently along at his side.

"I still see him," he replied after a pause. "He may have left for another ward two years ago, or he may have left for a while."

Over the next several weeks, Mr. Grey gave me a few more details about Dr. Sweetheart, including the "fact" that the charismatic doctor liked to keep track of his favorite patients by spying on them from the top of Building 2. Even when the doctor "left for a while," Mr. Grey was sure he returned at unpredictable but significant moments.

Mr. Grey himself had returned to the hospital at many unpredictable moments, and when I first met him he had already spent nearly eleven years in mental institutions. He had a reputation for talking "ragtime," as the schizophrenics' characteristic "word salad" was called at Mountain Valley, and I was not surprised that his accounts of Dr. Sweetheart were embellished with magic. But I was taken aback to discover that I could not rely on his memory for even the simplest information.

"Of course I remember Dr. Sweetheart," a physician's assistant said to me as she stopped in the corridor to shift a heavy stack of charts to her other hip. "He was a crazy little man—short and boxy with gray hair. He was slightly wall-eyed too, not attractive."

"But, Kathleen," I replied, somewhat aggrieved, "Mr. Grey tells me he was a little tall and handsome, with a lot of black hair. He said he wore a cape too and knew how to fly."

The white-jacketed Kathleen hiked the charts higher on her

hip as her gaze refocused on the past. She smiled. "I'd almost forgotten that. . . . Yes, Franklin came flying onto the ward one Halloween in a Superman outfit, complete with cape. He certainly did know how to fly."

Dr. Sweetheart's Superman caper was further confirmed by a social worker, but the latter clearly disapproved of such shenanigans and saw the doctor's unusually informal behavior in a different light. "I mean, he drank beer with the patients," he told me, shrugging hopelessly. "Unprofessional. I think he lived in a room off High Street."

"Down where the halfway houses are?" I asked, referring to the foster homes where we hoped to place many of the patients from 9-2-D.

"Exactly. I believe he liked that kind of life—being with the patients. Also, he was *not* a psychiatrist. He was a regular M.D. back from the army."

As I continued to gather curiously inexact information about Dr. Sweetheart, I found that my picture of him was beginning to split in two. In my mind's eye there was a funny-looking little doctor who cultivated unusual relationships with the patients, who did not work closely with the staff, and who, as several of my colleagues were hinting, could be vindictive. I also had an image of a slightly taller, wildly energetic doctor flying down the corridor of 9-2-D and perhaps leaping onto one of the brown chairs in the dayroom, his cape swirling around him. In my imagination I could see the broad smile that spread across Mr. Grey's face whenever the doctor's name was mentioned multiplied on a dozen other faces, and I suspected that Dr. Sweetheart may have connected with some of the most grievously ill patients in ways that few clinicians ever do.

Of course, I had heard of other charismatic doctors whom patients loved and staff mistrusted. One of my professors loved to tell of his own internship under a psychiatrist who cared for his patients like a doting and eccentric parent. When one of his psychotic patients was particularly distraught, this doctor would sit the patient on his lap and lovingly feed him dinner with a spoon.

"Unprofessional," admitted my professor, pausing to let us picture the little doctor holding his enormous child, "but if a member of my family ever had to be hospitalized, I'd want him on this man's ward."

Perhaps, I thought, a certain eccentricity or looseness was necessary for doing good work on the back wards, and I considered combining my pictures of the crazy and of the fantastic Dr. Sweetheart into a single image. But first I wanted to discover the simple facts of his life, such as whether or not he was a psychiatrist.

"Dr. Sweetheart was definitely a psychiatrist," said the ward psychiatrist a week or so later, as we reviewed Dallas Grey's voluminous chart. "He had a fondness for giving pedicures and performing minor foot surgery. It was part of his mystique."

"Did he live alone?" I asked, believing I already knew the answer but becoming less and less certain of what I heard.

"Oh my no. He was married to a very wealthy woman with an exceptionally loud voice. They had a brilliant daughter."

"Are you sure?"

"That she was brilliant?"

"No, that he was married."

"Of course. I used to call him at home, and his wife would shout at me over the phone."

And so it went. Whether I asked staff or patients, I always got answers that contradicted one another. I was told he was a regular physician and I was told he was a psychiatrist. For Mr. Grey, Dr. Sweetheart was tall and handsome. For the physician's assistant, he was short and boxy. He was married and had a brilliantly intelligent daughter. He was single and lived in a boardinghouse among patients. He spent all his time on the ward. He liked to rummage through hospital Dumpsters. He was still tucked away in some corner of the hospital or—and this was the only information that seemed reliable—he had left Mountain Valley some six or seven years before my arrival.

I kept the whimsical nature of memory in mind as I questioned Mr. Grey about his own life too. This diminutive and still boyish-looking man who cracked his knuckles, smiled nervously, and faded into the background at the slightest provocation, had been raised in Maine. He grew up in a family of four, he told me, five if you counted his great-aunt Tillie, but she had "the way" about her. When Dallas was three years old, his father had hit himself in the leg with an ax while splitting wood. He had bled to death before help arrived. His mother, a devoutly religious woman, wore black for the rest of her life. Although she never remarried, her husband's place was eventually filled by her brother-in-law, who was known as Uncle Sheriff or just Sheriff, apparently because of his strict discipline.

Both Dallas Grey's mother and his grandfather—the one who asked the young Dallas to get him two dozen doughnuts before he died—wanted Dallas to be a priest when he grew up. Uncle Sheriff wanted him to be "a real man." In addition, I learned that Bertie—whoever he was—gave Dallas a Christmas present every year which consisted of stolen money in a clean handkerchief, and an Aunt Noreen was a nun, who now lived in a foster home for people who were "mental." I wondered if Mr. Grey had given Dr. Sweetheart the same biographical bits and pieces as the two had gotten to know each other.

"Dr. Sweetheart would listen to you on the floor if you had something to say," Mr. Grey told me one afternoon, as we talked together on the ward. "He talked with me every day for five years. He said, 'Dallas, we have to cure you of contamination.'"

"What did he mean by that?"

"When I was in the army, they made me go pro. They said, 'Dallas, if you're going to be a man, you have to do it.' So they took me downtown and I said, 'OK, I get it. I'll do it.' And I did it."

"And did that contaminate you?" I asked.

Mr. Grey stared at his clasped hands. His normal expression of painful shyness gave way to serious concern, as if he were watching in his mind's eye the replay of a hazy, surrealistic dream that threatened even now to engulf him.

"What I remember is falling headfirst into a pit or a cesspool. Bang, bang! They grabbed me and I broke my arm. They said, 'Come back in nine months and we'll take you back.' So after they gave me the injections, I came to the hospital. Dr. Sweetheart said, 'We'll have to restore you to normal, Dallas.' And I said, 'I'm afraid of excommunication, but let's give it a try.' "

"So Dr. Sweetheart talked with you every day and tried to fix you up?"

"Yes," answered Mr. Grey with a weary sigh. "He started from the bottom up. He fixed my feet."

Over the next few days I made it a point to ask the nurses on the ward about the feet stories that kept cropping up at the mention of Dr. Sweetheart. I learned that he had, in fact, kept the patients' feet in excellent condition, but in so doing he had prompted the resignation of at least several nurses.

Apparently, Dr. Sweetheart experienced sizable ups and downs in his moods. His low spirits caused no memorable concern, but his highs drove the nurses to distraction. When he flew onto the ward and with tireless energy requested that ten patients be prepared for minor foot surgery in a single day, the nurses complained. They did not have enough buckets for ten foot soaks, and they were too shorthanded to clean up the water that spilled during these procedures. Dr. Sweetheart's response, I was told, was to write orders for not ten, not twenty, but twenty-four foot soaks BID—twice a day—and if the nurses did not comply he had an ace up his sleeve that no one wanted to see him put on the table.

According to legend (meaning according to Kathleen and a nurse *and* a social worker), Dr. Sweetheart used his ace only once. For reasons that have long since been forgotten, Dr. Sweetheart found himself embroiled in a particularly acrimonious power struggle with the nursing staff. They did not care for his patients with ardor. He pocketed all their ballpoint pens. They still withheld enthusiasm. He retaliated with foot soaks. Still they would not be moved. And so it is said that Dr. Sweetheart strode onto the ward early one morning, piled the patients' charts onto a gurney, and wheeled them into his office. One by one he opened them to the green page with DOCTOR'S ORDERS printed across the top, and there he rewrote the prescriptions for every single patient. He changed the medications themselves; he changed tablets to liquids (or vice versa); he changed the schedule of administration. And because he was nearly crazy with anger, it was said that he rescinded the "PRN" or "as needed" orders for major tranquilizers and sedatives. With this last maneuver, he removed the "chemical restraints" that modern hospitals rely on. In short, he ensured four days of absolute chaos.

"Tell me, Mr. Grey," I asked, as again I drew the job of returning him to the greenhouse, "did Dr. Sweetheart give you special medications for your troubles?"

"He prepared the medicines and Pookie Hauptmann gave them to me. 'Dallas, just take your medicine,' he would say."

"I mean did Dr. Sweetheart ever change your medicine?"

"They talk to you every day for two years. Then they cure you. It's a little surprise they have for you at the end."

"And what did you do when you were cured?" I asked, feeling it would be useless to question him further on medications.

"I went out in the snow and met Rosa. She had been in the hospital too and I went with her for a year. We were engaged and it ranged from good to extraordinary, but it wasn't like the one after the army. It wasn't infinity."

Mr. Grey was quiet for a long time as we walked up the steep hill toward the back of the hospital grounds. "You're mental, Dallas,' my uncle said to me then. 'You can't think fast and straight, and you can't pronounce words right since the second grade. You're not going to make it.'

"That was a big one for me too," he continued. "They grabbed me from behind and I fell headfirst into a pit. I broke my arm. But they broke me into the code too and made me go pro. I had to do it. They pushed me onto the ground and slugged me. They said, 'This is the way it goes, Dallas.'"

"And after that?"

"Eleven years on a locked ward," he replied with a shrug, "and fifteen minutes on an open one."

Over the next six months I pieced together Dallas Grey's history as best I could. When I asked him for clarification or details, he embroidered every incident with the reluctant seduction of a woman followed by punishment at the hands of a strong and sadistic man. The punishment usually involved falling into a hole and breaking his arm. The only other persistent memory he seemed to have was of being rescued by Dr. Sweetheart.

Mr. Grey had indeed been raised in Maine, as he claimed, and the hints he had dropped suggesting family turmoil were understated. The great-aunt who lived with the family was mentally ill, an Uncle Bertie had been imprisoned, then institutionalized, and Mr. Grey's live-in and supposedly law-abiding uncle was run out of town for impersonating a real sheriff and making arrests. In addition, Dallas Grey's brother spoke to pieces of kindling wood when he drank, as had his father before him. Thus it seemed fair to surmise both that Dallas Grey grew up in a turbulent household and that he was more than usually vulnerable to mental illness by way of genetic inheritance.

In addition, Dallas was apparently caught in an ongoing struggle between his uncle and his mother as well as between warring factions within his uncle's vengeful nature. The Sheriff raged at Dallas to become a real man and was particularly incensed when Dallas's mother countermanded his orders and made her son promise to become a priest. At times Mrs. Grey would baby her youngest son, which was reported to infuriate the Sheriff further still. When he was sufficiently angry, the Sheriff's punishing side may have expressed itself in physical abuse, although only Dallas's delusions remained to suggest the extent of the violence. His pervasive memories and delusions of forced love—going pro—and physical punishment implied to me that, at the very least, he was given intensely ambiguous messages about his sexuality, and that he was punished in one form or another for both the commission and the omission of manly acts.

Memory after memory of abuse flowed from Mr. Grey's inconstant mind, and each gave me a distorted glimpse of his childhood years that I could not put together in a coherent way.

"The earliest memory I have is bleeding from the head and being told I was a breech birth," he once said, and added, "My dog died on the road right in front of us. Blood was running out of his mouth and his face was swollen."

On another occasion he said, "They started reading my mind. Just sucked the thoughts out and knew I was afraid. 'You have to do it to show them you're a man.' So the doctors wrestled me to the floor and broke my back. They said, 'This is the way it goes, Dallas.' "

At this point I tried to locate Dr. Sweetheart's sidekick, Pookie Hauptmann, both to see if she had been able to reattach these drifting shreds of memory to the original events in Mr. Grey's life and also to learn the truth about Dr. Sweetheart. What had really happened to Dallas Grey to produce such tenacious memories of punishment and injury? And what had Dr. Sweetheart really done to leave behind such an ambiguous reputation?

Like many of the "old-timers"—staff who had been at Mountain Valley some fifteen or twenty years—Nurse Hauptmann had apparently moved from ward to ward. She had been around when Mountain Valley had been run like a big family, one of the gym teachers told me. There was less pressure and less paperwork then, he continued. A lot of staff left when the hospital expanded and became more professional. Maybe she had left then too.

As with Dr. Sweetheart and Dallas Grey, I was given bits of information about Pookie Hauptmann that did not fit together very well. It was suggested that she was an "older" nurse and that she was probably calm and genuinely caring. The gym teacher thought she had helped a great many patients in addition to Mr. Grey. I began to suspect that this vague description drew more on the staff's stereotyped idea of "the good nurse" than it did on Pookie herself, especially since warm and caring did not match Mr. Grey's current taste in caregivers. Over the past seven or six months, as he might have said, he had quietly developed a crush on a young nurse with straight blond hair and a no-nonsense approach to the patients. Demonstrative she was not, but there was a reticence about her, almost a seclusiveness, that apparently appealed to the quiet Mr. Grey. In any case, no one I encountered gave me specific details about Pookie Hauptmann, and only Mr.

Grey felt he knew for sure just where she was living now, namely, in prison.

"It was a mercy killing," he explained matter-of-factly. "She killed Louie because he was too short to live. She said good-bye and went to Newtondale."

Although I had learned nothing of value about Pookie Hauptmann, the exercise of trying to piece together her identity had taught me to be wary of the stereotypes, such as "the good nurse" or "the crazy doctor," that my informants apparently fell back on when memory failed. In fact, it seemed possible that a good nurse at Mountain Valley would eventually be credited with every good deed ever performed at the hospital and that an eccentric doctor would inadvertently be given bizarre details from other lives. For example, early on I was told that Dr. Sweetheart may have been the doctor who took one bite out of every sandwich he could get his hands on. This became such a problem on 9-2-D that the staff began hiding their lunches in bandage boxes, under the prescription pads, or in the sleeves of their overcoats. Predictably, three or four of the best-hidden lunches were lost each year, only to be found months later. In addition, Dr. Sweetheart attracted to his curriculum vitae the peculiar practice of dropping popcorn into people's coffee cups. Eventually I concluded that the sandwich and the popcorn stories belonged to two other psychiatrists. However, a fondness for pocketing pens, candy bars, and disposable slippers apparently belonged to Dr. Sweetheart.

Similarly, it was not always possible to piece together the events of Dallas Grey's life without confusing his deeds with those performed by other patients. For example, an aide told me of a series of suicide attempts that had spread through the ward like a twenty-four-hour grippe, but he was not sure just which patients had "followed the leader" in the attempts to jump, hang, slice, and sleep. Dallas might have been one. Nor were family members much more specific. Each had constructed a different life for Dallas Grey.

In spite of such drawbacks, I learned that Mr. Grey had enlisted in the army at age nineteen and left home. He was stationed in the South, and for three years did so well that he was recommended for Officer Candidate School training. In his third year he met a girl who worked at a nearby diner and had a brief affair. Unfortunately, he contracted gonorrhea, and one of the first signs of his impending breakdown was the growing belief that everyone could see that he was a contaminated man. Next, Mr. Grey became preoccupied with the idea that his bunkmate was interested in the same woman. This may have triggered memories of competing with his uncle for his mother's attention, and perhaps Mr. Grey expected his comrade to react with a similar anger. In any event, Mr. Grey ended the affair.

The waitress had been his first girlfriend, however, and the pain both of leaving her and of resurrecting childhood memories precipitated in this vulnerable man a psychotic break. Mr. Grey was treated in army hospitals for over six months before being discharged. He lived at home for several months. The following December he became depressed, and, on the anniversary of his first breakdown, he took a bus into the city and found himself a call girl.

"This was the best it has ever been for me," said Mr. Grey to his tightly folded hands. "It was better than Rosa."

"How long did you stay together?"

"Oh, an infinity. All evening."

"And then?"

Mr. Grey would not say, but an admission sheet filled out in the early-morning hours before Christmas told me that he had tried to kill himself with sleeping pills.

Mr. Grey was admitted to the hospital, and over the next several years spent an increasing proportion of his time in institutions. Finally he arrived at Mountain Valley and was assigned to a ward supervised by Dr. Sweetheart. The two saw each other daily for several years, and, with the doctor's encouragement, Mr. Grey made his last major attempt to live an ordinary life. He left the hospital, got a job, and became engaged to a former patient. The voices and the fears returned, however, and a badly demoralized Mr. Grey was readmitted.

At this point the entries in Mr. Grey's records begin to

change. Reports of assault become common; then those describing attempted suicide creep in. After slipping off the ward a dozen times, and each time trying to kill himself first by ingesting an entire dispenser full of Pez candies—the closest he could come to sleeping pills—then by throwing himself in the fish pond, he was transferred to a special ward for difficult or "at-risk" patients. There he would not have seen Dr. Sweetheart often, yet his memories insisted that the doctor was still around if you knew where to look.

Checking into the whereabouts of Dr. Sweetheart, I discovered that just at the time Mr. Grey was becoming unmanageable, the doctor was leaving Mountain Valley by degrees. As one story had it, the hospital gave him so much work that he finally asked to retire. Another version had the administration objecting to his policies and insisting that he retire. In either case, the doctor who flew through the corridors and took good care of his patients' feet, the doctor who befriended patients and aggravated staff, and the doctor who pocketed all the pens but probably did not drop popcorn into people's coffee, finally agreed to step down. But that was not the end of the story.

Dr. Sweetheart had two reasons for returning now and then to Mountain Valley. For one thing, his favorite patients needed him, and for another he needed pens. How he managed to follow the progress of certain patients like Mr. Grey is a mystery, but it was rumored that the doctor would simply appear on the hospital grounds, let himself onto the wards, and rewrite doctors' orders. He gave his patients what he thought they ought to have. Apparently, ward psychiatrists were enraged, and finally word went out that anyone who spotted Dr. Sweetheart was to call the security guard and have him ushered off the grounds. Both the social worker and the physician's assistant were quite sure that Franklin Leroy Sweetheart was last seen on a Sunday afternoon standing in the blue Dumpster outside Building 9 looking for discarded pens. He departed from Mountain Valley for good then and left behind both a caricature of a disobedient maverick and an image of a taller, black Superman poised for flight atop an enormous Dumpster.

Some six or seven years after Dr. Sweetheart finally left the hospital, Mr. Grey developed a medical problem that inadvertently pitted the painful, punishing memories of childhood against his good memories of Dr. Sweetheart. The occasion for this battle was a biopsy scheduled for December 26, which required that Mr. Grey be transferred to a medical ward on Christmas Eve.

About four o'clock that dreary afternoon I walked onto the garishly decorated ward to find Mr. Grey for a final talk. Outside it was almost dark, but on the ward itself a plastic Christmas tree was being lit in the nurses' station and the patients were jangling with uncommon excitement. A party was planned for that evening, and already trayloads of cakes and cookies were arriving from the community. Because the ward's meeting room was being used to store this food, Mr. Grey and I slipped into the dining hall. The usually austere tile-and-formica hall was crisscrossed now by red and green streamers, and on the walls foil snowflakes weakly reflected the winter light.

We sat down on either side of a long dining table. Mr. Grey folded himself up into a tiny bundle and would not speak. As I had noticed before, he had a way of retreating into his own thoughts so completely that he seemed to dematerialize. He was doing that now—disappearing right in front of me—and I was afraid that in his imagination he was turning a disagreeable medical procedure into a veritable nightmare. I remembered that when he had been caught smoking, he had expected aides to burn him, and when he was scolded for being late for his job, he believed he would be tortured.

"What are you thinking, Mr. Grey?" I asked.

"Nothing."

"Are you worried about the procedure they are going to perform?"

"No."

"Mr. Grey," I said, making an effort to sound businesslike, "tell me what your voices are saying."

"They've got me," he finally replied, still staring down into his baggy sweater. "They tell me I'll be strapped in. I can't have any food or water for three days. They'll put me down in the cellar where the bags, the red bags come out." Mr. Grey began to shake. "The doctors will come with their knives and cut open my rectum."

"Wait, Mr. Grey. . . . Listen to me." In the second or so that I had to plan and launch a counterattack against those powerful expectations of abuse, I recalled all the torturous memories that Mr. Grey associated with Christmas—his fragile loves, his break-downs, his persistent desire to sleep forever. I recalled too how powerless I felt when arguing against voices that were lodged so deep in his mind that they were closer to him than anything except, perhaps, other memories.

"It is true that you will be off the ward for three days," I began tentatively.

"Strapped down. Pushed into a pit."

"No. No pits."

"No food. No water."

"Mr. Grey, look at me. Three years ago you had a big opera-tion. Do you remember?" I had him looking at me now. I raised my voice. "You had your gallbladder removed. It was painful, but you survived. You got better."

"No."

"How did you get through that operation?" I asked, ignoring his answer.

"I didn't."

"Don't you remember how your stomach burned and you couldn't sleep?"

"Yes," he finally admitted, "I knew they were going to throw me down and burn the badness out of my stomach. But it never happened."

"But you had the operation and you got better," I insisted.

"No. Dr. Sweetheart took care of it. He put red ants down my throat and said, 'Dallas, when you wake up you'll be OK. Just remember to take your medicines. He'd say that. 'Just remember to take your medicines.' "

"Did you see him then?" I asked, knowing for sure that Dr. Sweetheart had gone by that time, but wondering if Mr. Grey had managed to wish his image right onto the medical ward.

"No. They tell me I was asleep, but he could see me. He can look down from the roof anytime."

"Mr. Grey, look at me," I said again. "How can we stop those voices? What would help you now?"

Dallas Grey emerged far enough from his sweater to stare out the window. His whole body was shaking in anticipation of yet another trip to hell.

"What would help?" I repeated.

"Medicine," he whispered. "Just remember to take your medicine, Dallas."

"Dr. Sweetheart!" I fairly shouted, finally realizing that the doctor's comforting presence was struggling to break into Mr. Grey's consciousness. "That's Dr. Sweetheart talking. Mr. Grey, I'm going to get you the medicine that Dr. Sweetheart would want you to have right now."

Dallas Grey nodded and slumped back down in his seat. I was not sure he was shaking less, but I thought so. As I hurried down the corridor to the nurses' station, I wondered at the mysterious ways of memory. Although Mr. Grey seemed unable to prevent many events from transforming themselves into sadistic tortures, he could occasionally rescue himself by conjuring up more benign delusions based on the real affection he had felt for Dr. Sweetheart.

But could he do this again after so many years? Could he do it for the rest of his life? Or was the flying image of Dr. Sweetheart gradually losing its power against those deep memories of violence that still colored so much of his experience? I doubted that I would get an answer to these questions any more than I had gotten answers to so many of my questions about Dallas Grey and Dr. Sweetheart. I asked a nurse for Mr. Grey's sedative and tried to resign myself to the increasingly familiar state of not knowing.

But I did know, I suddenly realized, as the charge nurse and

I dodged behind the Christmas tree and unlocked the pharmacy. The ability to comfort and be comforted resided both in the fantastic Dr. Sweetheart, who loved his patients "like a father and a son" and whom I now pictured with conviction as a crazy and wonderful doctor, and in the fantastic Mr. Grey, who was at that very moment, I hoped, performing the trick of a lifetime by holding on to that love long after Dr. Sweetheart had flown from Mountain Valley.

Testing the Pressured Brain

As I continued to work at the places that together I am calling Mountain Valley Hospital, I started on my doctoral dissertation. The topic was memory. I wanted to know if delusional patients—say a man who believed himself to be a space alien or one like Dallas Grey who was preoccupied with imminent torture—could remember. Could such individuals recall a story or a list of words that I read to them? Or could they recall only the tales they fabricated themselves? Most particularly, could a man like Matt Franklin, who claimed he was born as Jack London and was equipped with a mechanical brain and a pressure brain, remember which of his memories came from the "real" world of Mountain Valley and which from his far-ranging imagination?

The ability to recall where memories come from bears the somewhat pretentious label *reality monitoring*. In simplest terms this refers to the process whereby we tag certain events as being experienced and others as being imagined. Days or weeks later we are able to think back to the original event and remember not only some of the details but also whether the event actually occurred or we were merely daydreaming or anticipating. Most individuals keep track of the real and imagined portions of their lives very well, but I was not sure the same holds true for schizophrenics. Thus I proposed to test reality monitoring among delusional schizophrenics, both to see how well they could remember in general and to see if they could distinguish memories of what they had done from memories of what they had thought or imagined.

In the laboratory, the ways we have of measuring whether an individual can distinguish memories of doing from memories of imagining are heartbreakingly crude. To design a test that a patient can complete and a computer analyze, it is necessary to renounce the memories of cigarette-smoking dinosaurs and spangled prostitutes and turn instead to the simple task of reading words. The reading aloud of words stands in (we hope) for experience-in-the-world, and thinking words silently represents the process of imagining or thinking. Thus as a test of reality monitoring, a subject is asked to read a word aloud then read one silently, then aloud, then silently, and so on through thirty flash cards. After every ten cards he is handed a recognition sheet with twenty words on it, and he must underline the words he has said and circle the ones he has thought. Although several subjects from the schizophrenic and comparison groups came close to recalling all thirty words they had seen, none was able to remember precisely which he had read aloud and which he had thought silently. On average, members of the comparison group made reality-monitoring errors about 30 percent of the time. The schizophrenics did significantly worse.

Armed with this apparently simple but actually quite frustrating test, I set up "laboratories" both in the meeting room on Ward 9-2-D—that small, stuffy room with the abandoned exercycle—and in a similar room on 9-2-C. In the former, I would be testing Dallas Grey, Mr. Nouvelle, and about a dozen other patients already familiar to me. On 9-2-C, I would be testing strangers.

My first five or six patients presented only minor difficulties. Several insisted on signing the consent form with outrageous aliases, one was preoccupied with green plums which he felt were lodged in his ears, and a third gave me an endless account of higher education received from space aliens and delivered in classrooms that blinked and floated over the countryside like UFOs.

After I had administered thirty common words to each of these subjects, my delivery was smooth, and I thought I had learned to capture and recapture my subjects' wandering attention. When the fire alarm went off in the hall or when a subject began inscribing figures in the air, I just rolled along, flashing a "say" word and then a "think" word and so on.

"Mr. Franklin," I began, addressing a stiffly attentive patient about whom I knew nothing save that he was a forty-five-year-old paranoid schizophrenic of average intelligence. "Mr. Franklin, I would like you to read out loud each of the words—"

"Octavia!" he interrupted, drawing back in his chair as if stunned. "Octavia, I knew you in fourth grade and my dear" and here his voice became very low—"I have ne-ver for one in-stant ceased to use my pressure brain to give you and the entire ward feelings of the utmost bliss and joy."

"Thank you, Mr. Franklin," I replied, still holding the flash card in front of me. "Now what I'd like you to do is—"

"Relax in the flowing green light," he continued, finishing my sentence for me. "Rest in the soft green light of the Holy Spirit."

After explaining to me how he was, in truth, Jack London and had been born with the latter's pressure brain along with his own mechanical brain, the slight, dark-haired Mr. Franklin settled down to read aloud and think silently the words I presented. He sat across the table from me, rigidly upright, and acknowledged each word with a sharp bob of his small, rather boyish-looking head.

Halfway through the test Mr. Franklin closed his eyes and, to my dismay, began producing words of his own. Abruptly his pressure brain took over. He tightened his face as if blowing up a balloon and began grunting and puffing. Soon he was roaring as if about to explode.

"Mr. Franklin!" I shouted in alarm.

"Don't worry, Sister," he replied with sudden composure. "I'm used to it. As the sacrificial lamb, I was in terrible pain, but let that be a blank in your mind or you would shed too many tears.

You see," he continued, noticing the puzzled look on my face, "the pain I feel enables a billion women to be true."

"True in what way?" I asked.

"Between their legs, of course."

Mr. Franklin finished reading and thinking my words, and, in spite of the interruptions, managed to recognize eighteen of the thirty words, only a few less than the other patients I had tested. However, he could not begin to recall which words he had said out loud and which he had thought silently.

"You'd make a good nun, Sister," he remarked, as he stood formally beside his chair, preparing to leave. "I call you Sister because you're pure. We knew each other in the past but not with . . . Well, not with the unspoken word. I'm not sure you're ready for that yet." He hurried on now, his hands still held stiffly at his sides. "By comparison I'm a dog. Yes, don't contradict me. I . . . am . . . a . . . dog. It's not my fault." And here he moved to the door. "It's not my fault, but I feel the pain."

Mr. Franklin disappeared through the door, and a familiar confusion swirled through my head. I could almost see the after-images of the agile duel he had been waging with his inconstant brain. Connected to no one, he imagined the most intimate connection, then veered away from his fantasy by turning me into a nun. He also punished himself for his moment of wishing by becoming a dog, then reversed himself and claimed to be blameless.

In a similarly confusing and ingenious manner, he performed a sleight of hand on the pain he experienced, which apparently he could not bear if it truly came for no reason and meant nothing to anyone. Other patients had described for me a sudden, fearful pressure when it seemed their heads were caught in a vise and their thoughts—like winds funneled through a narrow canyon—were sped up to an intolerable degree. They felt then that their brains would burst through their skulls and spray out in a final and complete disintegration. In calmer times, most of these patients worked out an intricate yet ultimately inadequate set of rituals to ward off these spells or, as Mr. Franklin had just done, tried to give the pain a purpose. Mr. Franklin apparently believed that the whole ward benefited from the pressure that he was able to transform from random misfortune to a soft green light that bathed us lucky, unknowing ones in the Holy Spirit. I had seen ordinary individuals transform physical pain into stranger gifts, and I did not think I knew enough to say that Mr. Franklin was wrong.

But how did all these imaginative transformations of pain and improbable blendings of our separate pasts affect his memory? As common sense would suggest, his ideas distracted him, and the words he was reading when anxiety touched off his pressure brain were the ones he least remembered. This was not a new discovery. Distractions of all sorts are notorious befuddlers of memory, especially of a schizophrenic's memory.

I found that I too was distracted, only for me it was the test itself that took my attention away from the patients. It was an odd sensation to leave unexplored a blinking spaceship and a pressure brain.

Luckily, not all my patients were as distractible as Mr. Franklin and I, and after testing five or six more subjects I began to suspect that the patients' ability to recognize words was essentially intact. Setting aside the ability to distinguish "say" words from "think" words for the moment and looking only at recognition memory, I found that my two groups of subjects were indistinguishable. Both the patients and the nonschizophrenic subjects, all of whom were of similar age, intelligence, and education, were "hitting" about twenty of the thirty target words on the recognition sheets.

This observation was somewhat surprising, for many psychologists believe that the memory of chronic, thought-disordered schizophrenics is so severely compromised that even a relatively simple recognition task is too difficult for them. In fact, since the 1970s it has become so popular among psychologists to focus on the difficulties that schizophrenics have in learning, abstracting, categorizing, and remembering that it is now common to refer to schizophrenia as an "information-processing disorder." This term is meant to suggest that the basic problem in schizophrenia is not a traumatic childhood or a seductive, rejecting mother, but a malfunction of the brain itself. Opinion is still divided as to the precise nature and location of the problem.

Although both my groups recognized the same number of words on average, there was a greater variation in performance among the schizophrenics. Some, like the silent and preoccupied Dallas Grey, recognized only thirteen of the thirty words. Similarly, Mr. Nouvelle said with annoyance that he was so distracted by his brother who was trying to hug him and knock the pencil out of his hand that he could not remember "those clean little words." On the other hand, there were thought-disordered patients with remarkable memories. One man recognized twenty-four words because, he said, "I slept with a woman who did crossword puzzles and I guess she put those words in my head."

Mr. Knott did equally well, but for a different—and much more logical—reason. Short, wiry Mr. Knott was eager to break the monotony of a dark winter day by taking my word test. Given a few words to practice on, this swarthy, wrinkled man with a thatch of coarse black hair said "chair" out loud, presumably thought "soldier" silently to himself, and then shouted, "No! I don't want to be a soldier in the electric chair. Not me!"

For an instant I was nonplussed. Then, raising my voice to match his, I bellowed, "Let's get these words *out* of here!"

I continued to administer the test by flinging each flash card over my shoulder as soon as Mr. Knott had read or thought the word. Thus he saw thirty words. With some he concocted short, alarming sentences, but at the sight of others he merely rolled his eyes as if elaborating to himself on their significance. Because the test was taken amid such tumult, I was surprised when Mr. Knott proved to have an excellent memory. Later, however, I realized that the patients who embedded the test words in a story, be it a fragment like the soldier in the electric chair or an elaborate creation using many words, were using a powerful mnemonic device known for millennia. When they saw the to-be-remembered words on the recognition sheet, the story they had concocted came back to them and with it the key words they needed to remember. This did not necessarily help them when it came time to distinguish words said aloud from those thought silently, however, and such was the case with both Mr. Knott and his wardmate Mr. Brunetti.

No one used storytelling to better advantage than cagey old Mr. Brunetti, and all his stories revolved around love.

"Let's talk about Jolinda," Mr. Brunetti said affably, as he lowered his heavy body into the chair opposite mine. "Let's talk about love and Jolinda and jet planes."

As frequently happened on the ward, it was difficult to know which parts of Mr. Brunetti's stories were true, in the usual sense of the word, and which imaginary, but in his case the essentials were well documented. For over fifteen years this slow-moving, rather shapeless man had been steadfastly in love with one of the female patients at Mountain Valley. Most of the time her name was Jolinda Muniz, and she was a short, sturdy-looking woman who wore coveralls. Occasionally, she was John Hines, a bomb builder for a secret government agency, but this, she explained, did not change her feelings for Mr. Brunetti. It merely made her vision so sharp that she saw the world as if through the wings of a fly.

Mr. Brunetti and Ms. Muniz first met when he was about fifty and she twenty-seven, and by the time I saw them the details of their early encounters had been washed away by Mr. Brunetti's torrential Italian imagination. What remained were memories of food. The two were drawn together, Mr. Brunetti recalled, by their common love of food. For years and years of Saturdays—in fact, as long as he could tolerate his arthritis and she her fallen arches— the two would walk a mile and a half into the neighboring town of Hillsdale and there purchase "a stack of meatball grinders three feet high." They would buy quarts of soda too, then lug their booty back up the valley to the hospital. On good days they would camp out for the entire day at the picnic tables under the maples behind Building 9.

"It was heaven," remembered Mr. Brunetti, smiling broadly. "Che bella donna. My wife-in-name-only and I would eat and doze and eat and doze. We'd lie on our backs and watch jet planes, and I would imagine whatever I wanted. Tutta cosa.

"I had a friend who owned a religious store send me and

Jolinda matching prayer books," he continued, and here he drew a red, leather-bound missal out of his pocket. "After that our feet got too tired to walk into town, so now we mainly sit on the benches."

For her part, Jolinda maintained that "her friend" was "OK." Yes, he gave her things, but nothing she couldn't get herself, and yes, she liked to sit with him on the benches because he never got fresh and no one bothered her when they were together. It was nice, she admitted, zipping and unzipping the side pockets on her coveralls, to have a friend who was older and weaker. She seemed oblivious to the fact that the two had become one of the legendary couples at Mountain Valley.

When I finally got Mr. Brunetti to alternately say and think my thirty words, I could hear him ebulliently incorporating them into what for me was an utterly nonsensical story about a sidewalk that rolled up as you walked along it and passionately took in boxes and rivers as it went along. Nevertheless, when I handed him the recognition sheets, he unerringly selected twenty-seven of the thirty target words, the best score that any subject in either group attained. The distinction between saying and thinking, however, had been entirely lost, and he assigned the words he recognized to those categories at random.

After testing my complete sample of twenty thought-disordered schizophrenics, I concluded that, bizarre as their thinking seemed to be, they were as capable of recognizing words as are ordinary individuals. Thus when a test of memory was short enough (or, in a less contrived situation, important enough) to hold their attention, the information entered their brains, was encoded, and later could be retrieved, at least when they were reminded of the words by seeing them again on a recognition sheet.*

---

*Psychologists make a distinction between the relatively easy process of recognition— seeing or hearing something *again* and identifying it as previously encountered—and the more difficult process of "free recall," which involves retrieving information from memory without reminders. Recognition is considered an automatic process. For example, it is almost impossible to see the letters y e s and not recognize the word *yes*. On the other hand,

But when it came to identifying which information—words, in this case—had been spoken aloud and which thought silently, most of the schizophrenics were in trouble. In fact, they averaged twice as many mistakes as did the subjects in the comparison group. Again there was considerable variation among the patients.

At the end of six weeks I had tested some forty subjects and had translated the information thus gathered into hundreds of numbers. I had my data. Quite to my surprise, however, I found I had acquired a different kind of information as well. Seeing a number of patients for only one hour and asking each of them to perform exactly the same task gave me a different perspective on schizophrenia than did talking with only a handful of patients for months on end. What struck me during testing was both their diversity and their seclusiveness.

The most obvious difference among the patients I tested at Mountain Valley was the degree to which they were willing to engage with other people. Nearly half my subjects sat silently across the table from me and willingly revealed almost nothing of themselves. At most they would hint obliquely at the nature of their preoccupations.

"If you walk through a door the wrong way, voices tell you to go back," one woman said with a sigh. "And if you walk through it right, then they tell you something else." That was all she offered.

"Patient cannot be placed in foster home at this time," I read in the chart of another silent subject, "due to his persistent attempts to set himself on fire."

"It's the electric voices," explained this slow, gentle-looking man, when I prodded him about his frightening compulsion. "They're so close in my head I can't ignore them."

These were the kinds of patients I saw crouched in the hallways or sitting dumbly in front of a television set. They did not appear to talk to anyone, and it was difficult to know if they were

---

free recall, which is involved in remembering what you ate yesterday for breakfast, for instance, is considered an effortful process.

even talking to themselves or hearing voices. (The most toneless and lethargic patients are said to suffer from the negative symptoms of schizophrenia.)

At the other end of the scale were the voluble patients, who apparently needed to make a smashing connection with everyone they encountered.

"I designed the bomb, you know," said Jolinda Muniz belligerently, as I tried to get her to say and think my words. "I did. I mean really. It's mine."

"Years of education?" echoed another, repeating my question. "Twelve. Twelve at the University of Michigan. Twelve at Purdue. University of Minnesota. Yale, Mannheim, the Sorbonne. . . ."

Within this somewhat invasive group of patients were men and women with unique preoccupations—"I have a worm farm, right here. In my stomach"—and those with the more common preoccupations of religion and sex. Like Matt Franklin and the Dinosaur Man, these patients dodged back and forth across the boundaries of authority and intimacy trying, it seemed to me, to express how much they wanted power and love and how afraid they were of getting them.

Superimposed upon the patients' level of sociability, however it was expressed, were other attributes, such as intelligence and insightfulness. Thus in testing I glimpsed patients who were affable, slow-witted, and utterly unaware of their condition—I am thinking of a man who apparently measured the years of his life solely by the car accidents he believed he had suffered along Route 1—and I met others who were remote, painfully aware of their predicament, and, to my astonishment, smart enough to do well on my word test and on the test of intelligence that I also administered. Had I not tested eight or ten of these withdrawn patients, I might have assumed that all quiet patients are slow-witted either by way of inheritance or from decades of mind-altering medications. Conversely, I might have assumed that all noisy patients are likely to be as incomprehensible as Paul Whitman, who, sashaying into the testing room with his T-shirt tied into a bolero, dramatically proclaimed himself to be "Magnolia."

"A woman's test!" he squealed, snatching one of the recognition sheets off the table before he'd even begun to read or think the words.

" 'Flower,' " he read. "Yes, I'll take flowers. 'Bread' is good too. But 'soldier'? No, no, no. Soldiers are for boys. And boys," he suddenly shouted, his voice deep and menacing, *"don't get pregnant!"* With that he clasped his hands over his crotch and shimmied out of the meeting room.

I could see then why some clinicians throw up their hands when it comes to considering schizophrenia as a single disorder with a common cause. Remote, vociferous, logical, delusional, predictable, unpredictable, dull, or imaginative, the patients on 9-2-C and D seemed to suffer from a whole family of only loosely related disorders. The only traits they seemed to share were an emotional circuitousness that almost guaranteed that what they said was not exactly what they meant and a disconnectedness that at some level, I believed, was related to their difficulty in distinguishing *say* from *think* and *do* from *imagine*.

Returning to my numerical data, the similarity between the schizophrenic and comparison groups on the recognition portion of the task and the wide difference between the two groups on the reality-monitoring portion yielded two suggestions. First, the data implied what some psychologists have long suspected, namely that memory is not a single process but involves a variety of processes that are less intertwined than previously imagined. Some individuals may be good at some aspects of remembering and poor at others. Too often the right answers on a memory questionnaire involve three or four distinct processes, and when a subject gives wrong answers his or her mistakes are interpreted as demonstrating an overall deficit or problem. Thus in the case of delusional schizophrenics, it would not be fair to conclude that just because some of them cannot distinguish what they ate for lunch from what they imagined they ate, these individuals have no capacity for remembering. Some, like Messrs. Brunetti and Knott, certainly do.

The second generalization that my data supported is that thought-disordered schizophrenics can handle information processing that is automatic (like recognizing words they have already seen) but have trouble with "effortful processing," for which they have to push and prompt their memories along a trail of intermediate thoughts in order to arrive at the desired conclusion. Recollecting whether a word was spoken or thought requires this kind of search.

In an attempt to explain more concretely why schizophrenics are such poor monitors of reality, I examined the association between their reality-monitoring scores and their IQ, education, age, and even degree of thought disorder. I found none of these factors to be correlated with either very good or very poor reality-monitoring scores. There was a hint of a correlation that intrigued me, however, and this was between reality monitoring and a peculiar quality of memory which, alas, I had not specifically set out to investigate.

During the time I spent on 9-2-D, I had often wondered why the stories that schizophrenics told me were so haunting. Why did space aliens that communicate by burping through their ears or the soft green light of the Holy Spirit lodge themselves so firmly in my mind? One afternoon, as I listened to a wonderful story about a worm farm that a patient was certain existed in his stomach and that he cared for by eating twice the amount of food he needed, I realized that certain patients told me stories in ways that made them easy to remember. They told me their stories in so ambiguous a way that I had to reorganize the material in order to understand it at all, or they actually included me in their personal memories, as a fellow fourth-grader, for example, or as a wife in a former lifetime. Either of these presentations forced me to participate in their stories to a much greater degree than one is usually asked to do.

Scientifically speaking, this participation made the stories easy to remember by means of a process called the self-generation effect, which, in the simplest terms, asserts that we remember information we have actively helped to produce much better than material we have simply listened to. For the schizophrenic, however, this habit of incorporating others into his personal past blurs the boundaries between teller and listener as well as between past and present. As one would expect, monitoring reality under these conditions is difficult, and of the four patients who seemed most anxious to capture my attention by creating what might be called parasitic memories, three had the poorest scores on the reality-monitoring portion of my test.

Thus, as so often happens, when the time came to pull my observations together, I could state with confidence what I had initially suspected, that even though my schizophrenic subjects were able to recognize material they had seen, most found it diffi-cult to remember where it came from. But I could only hint at what I *seemed* to have discovered, namely that those patients whose delusions characteristically mixed past with present and self with others were particularly handicapped in distinguishing what had actually happened from what they may have imagined. This did not seem like a great deal of information to have acquired by chasing subjects around the ward for six weeks, but I knew that the precise nature of my findings would emerge only after I had woven my observations into the fabric of other psychological experiments. The best part, the testing, was just the beginning.

Several years have passed since I tested pressured brains for my dissertation, and I have all but forgotten most of the numbers and many of the names. But I have not forgotten the storytellers— the Dinosaur Man, the keeper of the worm farm, or Matt Franklin, who knew me in fourth grade as Octavia. Thinking back, I find that it is more difficult for me to say now whether these men were the most handicapped, with so weak a hold on reality that they could not even tell where they stopped and I began, or whether they were also (or instead) the least inhibited in trying to make up for the hundreds of common connections that were missing from their lives. Perhaps the patients with the poorest reality-monitoring scores had a somewhat easier time expressing feelings that elude most rational individuals, namely feelings that one is connected to places or even to strangers in deeper ways than the facts of the matter can fully explain. I am not arguing that schizophrenics are more sensitive than their doctors or that they are psychics in disguise. I am suggesting only that what might appear under ordinary circumstances to be a dysfunctional way of keeping track of experience—a reality-monitoring problem—may, in extremis, be a method of staying afloat.

The artist Arshile Gorky once wrote that art must "force the viewer to contribute something of himself in order that he extract as much as possible out of the particular work." In a curiously similar way, certain delusional patients seem bent on forcing their listeners to contribute portions of their own pasts so that both can share an immediate, albeit unusual connection. In the case of the artist and his viewers, Gorky asserted that a joint effort leads to a deep and thoughtful understanding of their common nature. And for schizophrenics and their listeners? For sacrificial lambs and fourth-grade students? Perhaps when the pressured brain ensnares a willing listener, a connection—although not precisely the one imagined by Mr. Franklin—is made, and, as with any real connection, there may come with it an exchange of understanding and respect.

How They Live on the Moon

Whatever you invent is true, even though you may not
understand what the truth of it is.

GUSTAVE FLAUBERT

What I have never seen discussed in the scientific literature on delusions is their considerable allure. When I arrived on the back wards of Mountain Valley Hospital, I already knew that delusions are among the most common, intriguing, and poorly understood phenomena in psychopathology, and I knew too that rival theories had been proposed to explain their occurrence among the emotionally disturbed. But I was unprepared for their charm. Where, I wondered, was the paper that investigated delusions not as symptoms but as stories which, whether well wrought or drab, grandiose or grim, are all messages set adrift from the shores of a cunningly unreasonable world?

At first I believed that to fall under the spell of these tales was a personal indulgence, or worse, but even before I knew enough to justify my susceptibility, I'd been captured by the story of a university run by space aliens, by a man who sang himself to the moon, and by a woman's apocryphal memories of a retarded, albino son who daily performed feats of astounding devotion.

In my first months on the back wards, I did not think of delusions as stories. Defined by psychologists as implausible beliefs that are firmly held, idiosyncratic, and utterly lacking in social validation, the delusions I heard were too fragmented to tell me much.

"When they brought him back from the dead they gave him a small body," a patient said to me, pointing toward a short psychiatrist who had, indeed, been out sick.

"Space aliens communicate by burping through their ears," another said to me several times, with what seemed to be a complicitous wink.

"My little toe took me walking around the world."

"And then?" I would ask. "And then?" But the speakers would rarely elaborate on demand, and I could not tell whether these thoughts were isolated ideas or pieces of a larger cosmology. Gradually, however, I made out that patients carrying a wide variety of diagnoses—from schizophrenia to manic-depressive to Huntington's chorea—had an equally wide variety of delusions, although no specific type of fantasy was uniquely associated with a single disease. Some patients had grimly simple scenarios, such as eat food and you will be poisoned, and others had richly embroidered tales of staggering complexity. Some had delusions of grandeur, such as being a great boxer surrounded by movie stars all impersonating nurses, but most had paranoid delusions and felt threatened by torture and death. But simple or complex, restricted to one aspect of life or global, great or gruesome, the delusions on Ward 9-2-D began to hold together more as I learned to listen. They sounded more and more like stories to me, and as stories they varied most noticeably along two dimensions. One was their usefulness—to their creators—and the other was their artfulness or appeal to the listener.

Some of the simplest delusions, limited in both these categories, concerned improbable illnesses. A calamity such as being bombarded by plums apparently protected Mr. Clauson from the greater dangers of psychotic rage. A slight man with a springy gait, he was frequently seen hurrying down the hall, wads of cotton protruding from his ears. Other times he would squint as if trying to protect his eyes. The cotton, he told me, was to prevent green plums from getting into his ears and growing there, and the squinting, he admitted, was an ineffectual attempt to stop dirt from being sucked into his nervous system.

Mr. Clauson's unusual illnesses came and went with remarkable speed, and as I listened to him talking with other patients I could see that when he got into a disagreement he would often frown angrily for a moment, then turn his attention to a symptom.

"There are only trains of thought that sharply sound aware," I once heard him snap when accused of hearing voices, and with that he clapped his hands over his ears and charged off toward the nurses' station in search of cotton.

As useful as his delusions may have been in deflecting rage or as important as they may have been for other reasons, no one on 9-2-D was particularly interested in Mr. Clauson's plums. Because delusions were understood to be caused by a chemical imbalance in the brain that, among other things, scrambles fearful fantasies with actual experience, the treatment of choice was the restoration of a healthy chemical balance by means of medication. Even though this treatment has proved effective in only about two out of three cases of schizophrenia, medicines were considered much more helpful (and much quicker) than any amount of discussion concerning the delusions themselves. Thus when I told the ward psychologist that Dallas Grey was letting me in on "the code" that signaled for him the onset of torture, it was suggested that I tell him, "We don't speak code in this hospital. When you're ready to talk my language, I'm ready to listen." This was intended to teach Mr. Grey that crazy talk drives people away—a useful lesson.

From my point of view, however, the most interesting parts of the patients' lives were precisely their delusions. For one thing, it was much more enjoyable to discuss delusions than, say, hygiene, because the patients themselves were clearly more interested in the worlds spinning silently in their heads than in anything else. For them, keeping away from the vicious "Arabies" or courting the occidental ladies was the essential business of the day. For another thing, talking about delusions was more informative. I felt that tales of torture or greatness told me a great deal about how patients viewed the world of Mountain Valley, what they loved and hated and hoped for, and perhaps where they had come from as well. And last, ridiculous as it may sound, my interest in patients' delusions was a matter of habit. When someone leaned toward me and said, "Once my mother turned herself into a bee with compound eyes as large as plates," I automatically stopped whatever I was doing and listened, just as I had done as a child.

As a listener, one of the first things I noticed was that the longer a patient had been delusional *in adulthood*, the more likely it was that his fantasies had threaded their way back into his childhood. New delusions focused on hospital life. Old ones, like Ivana Goldman's, spiraled insidiously into both past and future.

Ivana Goldman was a towering, large-boned woman who, with skeins of gray hair literally tied in knots at the top of her head, inspired fear in all who encountered her. She had passed a considerable portion of her life going in and out of mental institutions on a roller coaster of moods, and, in or out, she was constantly shouting to her invisible companions. Her elderly mother said she could not care for Ivana because her daughter argued with her old business cronies even in her sleep.

Unlike the majority of delusions on the ward, which were persecutory in one dreadful way or another, Ms. Goldman's centered on greatness, and so pervasive and elaborate had they become that now they permeated every aspect of her life and every period of her past. She told me that when she was one year old and still in diapers she crawled into a temple and amazed the congregation by talking to them of serious matters. As a teenager she was a top executive at Young and Rubicam, and now, as a woman of about fifty, she was awaited by the president and his wife at the White House.

Ms. Goldman's stories of wheeling and dealing among executives were characteristically delivered in a whiskey baritone and accompanied by a lot of loud thumping on her attaché case, which was, in fact, a wooden box that had once housed a gift assortment of wines. Although her diatribes plowed into everyone with considerable force and wearing repetitiousness, her arguments were not without appeal. There was an earnestness in her scheme for introducing a crunchy new brand of children's cereal in the shape of dollar signs, for example, and a generosity in her insistent offers to share the profits that made her listeners want to like her. But the price of listening was often steep. When excited, Ms. Goldman would explode if a single detail of her scheme were challenged, nor would she stand for any level of enthusiasm in her listeners that was less than her own. Thus, when she lured someone into conversing, the ensuing exchange grew in volume like a high school ball game and, like these boisterous affairs, frequently ended in a free-for-all as the listener's "reality" ran up against Ms. Goldman's squad of intractable delusions. Even in calmer moments, when she herself felt the facts of the outside world skulking along the edges of her mind, she would admit only to little things, like being loud, before returning to her dreams. But the most curious aspect of Ms. Goldman's seamlessly constructed world was her creation of an absolutely silent child.

As the story went, Ms. Goldman had come upon the mute and severely retarded boy in a home for runaways and had adopted him in spite of his disabilities. The toddler was immediately overcome with gratitude; indeed, every story about the strange platinum-haired child had as its twin subjects the boy's devotion and Ms. Goldman's amazing tolerance and understanding.

"He loves me," she would say, shaking her disheveled head in disbelief. "He adores me. I've been so good to him. I miss him now. . . ." And here Ivana Goldman's voice would mellow, and her story would totter off into the interstices of her mind at a more relaxed pace. There, in her imagination, we might come upon a fabricated memory of the slim, white-skinned child sitting on her lap, wordlessly conveying his devotion, or on one of the boy learning a simple but endearing task, such as licking the flaps of envelopes for an important mailing.

Although I knew enough about Ms. Goldman's past—including her years in Queens, which was as close as she ever got to Madison Avenue—to feel certain there was no truth to her stories in the ordinary sense, the delusions struck me as uncannily apt. Her child was the perfect representation both of her own idealized identity—a person with a beautiful soul but with no ordinary way of expressing himself—and of her idealized opposite and partner. The son remained young as Ms. Goldman got old. The boy was compact and fair, Ms. Goldman was dark and gangling. The former was mute, the latter never stopped talking. The child was retarded, his mother was bright. And, of course, the son was also a malleable male, a miniature masculine Pygmalion. In all the essential ways the two complemented each other, and neither had a complete identity without the other.

Having given herself so complete an identity, Ms. Goldman was at home in the world. Her delusions gave her very much the kind of station in life that an identity based on memories gives to other people. Like them, she knew how to treat the people around her and knew how she should be treated in return. Of course, no one acknowledged her self-proclaimed celebrity, and each of her imperious demands for a private plane or an audience with the president was ridiculed and rejected. And, curiously, this too was part of the usefulness of her delusions. The discrepancy between her view of herself and everyone else's view guaranteed a steady stream of misunderstandings and rejections which, in all probability, was what Ms. Goldman had been used to since early childhood. Especially because she took the rejection of her demands to mean not only that she should not have a plane but also that she should not ask to be seen as someone special, her delusional requests kept her punitive history on course. She felt doubly rejected every time she asked to be admired.

And this was not all. Ms. Goldman's delusional system also rescued her from boredom and, further still, explained her feelings of frustration and distress. These, she told herself, were not the result of anything like self-doubt but came from the staff's unwillingness to believe in her and her stories.

The disadvantage of Ms. Goldman's manner of living was that it disconnected her from others and from herself. As long as she lived in her imagination, she could not rejoin the people around her, nor was she likely to call her personal problems by their right names and begin to deal with them. Of course, this common method of circumventing real issues by focusing on something else—complaining of a partner's drinking problem rather than facing one's own reluctance to insist on sobriety, for example—is not unique to the delusional. Recently I had been given an admirable lesson in avoiding the feelings of confusion and sadness that accompany any real gain in self-understanding by a lonely bachelor who insisted that his only regret in life was being scratched by a cat he had tried to help down from a tree. The ungrateful animal had allegedly given him cat-scratch fever. Although this diagnosis was never confirmed by a physician, my client insisted that his entire fund of malaise was generated by this malady. Of course getting the fever was not his fault and curing it was not his responsibility.

Whether this kind of thinking is outright delusional or merely stubbornly wrongheaded, the point that the mislabelers of distress brought home to me was that, to a therapist, the fictions people live by are extremely useful as symbols that express their distress but are not directly useful in alleviating the problem. I could agree with the ward psychologist that, in and of itself, no amount of talking about cat-scratch fever or the need for a private plane was going to refocus my patients' attention on their loneliness or feelings of inferiority. But could the transition from discussing the external fiction to facing the internal concern be made by decree? I didn't think so. In any event, until such a transition was effected, little change would occur in the patient's life, and he or she would continue to live apart.

But this did not bother Ivana Goldman, who seemed unaware of what to others was a radical and unsettling independence. Her incredible stories kept life on an even keel. Her silent child did all that such an apparition can do for its creator. He was useful.

In terms of artfulness, however—that is to say, in terms of plots and subplots, monstrous characters, dazzling scenes, and the dextrous use of fantasy—Ms. Goldman's private mythology was only mediocre. Her stories overpowered but did not beguile. Although possessed of great energy, the aging businesswoman lacked the elasticity of mind to stretch her ideas around the common details of hospital life, nor did she have the wit to dazzle and bemuse. But the Dinosaur Man did.

A wonderfully eccentric man, Mr. Nouvelle had spent his entire adult life in mental institutions, and over the course of some thirty-seven years of hospital life, had fabricated a series of identities that extended from the Cretaceous to the present. Along the way he tried on good and evil, male and female, power and weakness. He had been everything except a plant or a rock, and now he lived as some dozen characters in a world in which, although he appeared to have no control over it, he specified every detail.

It was not easy to be sure just who this delicate, gray-haired man was at any given moment. Dressed in his curious blue uniform—half security guard or military and half Future Farmers of America—with thick glasses magnifying his mocking, gold-flecked eyes, he glided in and out of character as easily as he moved among the secret hiding places on the hospital grounds. In the good times, relatively speaking, he was God the Father, the son who never sucked dick, a doctoreate professor, or the Sophisticated Man. Under duress, he became Howitzer Bombardier, a Venetian soldier, the Inspector General, or a bum. And, when he drifted between these two extremes, he said he was a Nicodemosaurus with a small dinosaur mother and six dinosaur wives.

The schizophrenic Mr. Nouvelle did not suddenly find himself feeling and acting like a "doctoreate" or a dinosaur, as might happen to a person suffering from a split personality. These facets of his personality were more like aliases, and he adopted them in response to the situation at hand. At first I found it difficult to disentangle his delusional personae, but gradually I acquired a feel for the major transmogrifications of his spirit. Howitzer Bombardier, for example, embodied much of Mr. Nouvelle's rage. Once, when the Dinosaur Man learned from the cashier in the canteen that he was ten cents short and could not buy coffee, the Bombardier suddenly appeared and turned all the plates of spaghetti on the counter into mounds of bloody road-kill. At other times, Howitzer Bombardier would pace rapidly along the right-hand side of the long hospital corridors, one finger ticking lightly along the tiles. In his mind, he told me, he was killing everyone in sight with a machine gun. He was cutting them in half, leaving them to bleed. Now and again he would pick up his foot as if stepping over a body.

Other times, when he spotted a woman, for example, the situation called for a sophisticated man. As such, he would follow the woman with a stare so intense that most nurses were afraid of him. He needed to pay close attention, however, for by decoding her smallest gestures he could tell if she were making love and giving him, there in the corridor, an invisible moment of pleasure.

To say that Mr. Nouvelle could choose to embody a certain aspect of his character is misleading, as is the notion that he could regulate his flights of fancy. Unlike ordinary people, who are only occasionally beset by preoccupations so intense that the disturbing ideas cannot be chased from their heads, Mr. Nouvelle was always at the mercy of his ruminations. He had to run from the very thoughts he generated and was forever in danger of being betrayed by the very cleverness that he depended on to survive the chaos of schizophrenia.

"My other image robs me of such joy," he once said, obviously upset by something that had gone on in his head. "It cheats and tricks me. I was standing in line, about to blow a whole line of men, when the Arabies indooblecated me and queered the deal." Even when he was successful in snatching a moment of imaginary pleasure, his own fantasies exacted an unpredictable price.

One day, for example, Mr. Nouvelle burned his way through a group of student nurses with his stare but immediately complained of being put on trial. The story changed even as he told it—even as he went back in his "photographic imagination" to the scene of the crime. He had been sitting in the lobby of Building

9, smoking, he told me, when a girl in cutoffs came up to him. He touched her on the leg, and in an instant the lobby turned into a courtroom. For the twenty-eighth time he was accused of committing a crime.

"I'll tell you what I've done today," he remembered saying to the judge. "I slipped down to the Sunset Creamery for ice cream, where the black woman drops water down men's pants, *and did that girl think I punched her?!*"

Now the girl or nurse appeared, dressed in white. Mr. Nouvelle asked her to take off her clothes, and again he touched her on the leg.

"I was not sent to prison that time . . . , perhaps because I had the courage to show them," he said with a frown. "But when a woman acts like a child and won't mother a man, then she deserves to be punched."

With a shake of his head he came back to the present. "A man has a mind that rattles on so," he concluded. And certainly mine rattled as I attempted to parse his mythology and figure out how a man could feel sufficiently mothered without being treated like a boy or just who the desirable but unloving girl represented, either among the hospital staff or among his past relations. As with most of the delusions I heard, this fragment pointed both to private problems, possibly stemming from childhood, and to more general ones, such as how to be an autonomous adult and an obedient patient at the same time.

Like the problems the delusions expressed, the characters in them were also contemporary. There were no Napoleons on 9-2-D. Ours was a thoroughly modern collection of grown-up children, sinful lovers, powerless politicians, and impotent soldiers. Mr. Nouvelle had, in fact, created a caricature of twentieth-century turmoil in his head, and in this tumultuous drama he played some dozen starring roles while the staff, unknowingly, played supporting parts. Hospital aides became IBM maintenance men who rendered him literally obsolete by removing parts of his brain. Student nurses formed a harem of occidental wives condemned by God, and several male patients were really women in disguise. All of us were potent spoilers and seducers, yet our only power came from Mr. Nouvelle's grand and useless omniscience.

No turn of the head or touch of the face was made by a woman that the Sophisticated Man did not interpret. Nor was there any pattern of food on a lunch plate that the Inspector General could not decode. Conversely, Mr. Nouvelle believed that everyone who glanced at him as he ticked his way along the corridors could read his mind and see through his clothes. Sometimes they could even know his thoughts as these were broadcast for all to hear and condemn. In short, each actor in his delusional world could understand everything, explain everything, remember everything.

At first I thought that, like a novelist, Mr. Nouvelle had simply made us all know more than we could possibly know, and I rather enjoyed visiting his marvelously transparent world. But the Dinosaur Man was a novelist with no control over his plot and no ability to escape from his own ideas. His make-believe understanding resulted in a disagreeable lack of privacy and personal efficacy for him, and eventually I, too, felt this powerlessness. It was like watching too much news on television. My head was being stuffed with the intimate details of a world which I could not affect in any way. I could try to understand what the delusions stood for, but neither I nor Mr. Nouvelle could act upon this self-contained system any more than we could change the plot of a novel that someone else was writing.

So, like Ivana Goldman and dozens of others, Mr. Nouvelle was stuck. Daily he seemed to create his own world and endow himself with extraordinary powers, yet because his beliefs were not acted out in the company of others and modified by actual consequences, there was no real action on his stage. Women passed by with a smile or a frown, yet no one really fell in love or argued or comforted each other. His was a teeming, scrambling world which, upon closer inspection, appeared to be a frozen concoction in the mind—unreachable and unchangeable.

When I turned my attention from Mr. Nouvelle's characters to his plots, it came as no surprise to find them equally confusing, and in great measure it fell to the foolhardy listener to make them intelligible.

"I always give the dinosaurs a dollar and a quarter for Coca-Cola," he announced, and I tossed that meaningless distraction—or was it a Rosetta stone?—into the air where other references to Coke were already spinning. On another occasion, when he said, "I keep forcing down the Coke even when I'm full and I can tell by the look on the other man's face that he really wants my Coke," I was reminded of my first days on the ward, when I had seen him downing invisible cans of soda. Since then I had accumulated in my mind hundreds of strange symbols and relics that never quite fit together. I had nouns and verbs but no conjunctions. And being so incompletely informed, I wondered if I had the right to set myself up as the interpreter of his stories. Did I know enough to say, for example, "No, you aren't telling me a story about dinosaurs and Coke, you're telling me that Mother's milk was in short supply in your family"? Did anyone know enough to say, as I sometimes heard, "Your ideas are symptoms of your illness. They don't mean anything at all"?

The answer to this problem of interpretation seemed to vary with the day. Sometimes Mr. Nouvelle would not tolerate any interpretation at all and became furious if I hinted that my dinosaur identity might be a way of expressing feelings of kinship. Absolutely not. On other occasions I could treat his delusions as symbols as long as I kept very close to the feelings they conveyed. Thus statements such as "I don't like it when I am treated like a boy, yet too much emphasis is put on being a banana" could lead to a discussion of the privileges and responsibilities of adulthood versus childhood.

Most of the time, however, my interpretations proceeded much less smoothly. Like other patients, Mr. Nouvelle had learned to guard his delusions carefully, and although he might swerve into my world for a minute or two, he quickly bolted back to his own if I tapped too insistently on the wall of his ideas.

For example, the day after Mr. Nouvelle had watched the Super Bowl on TV, I agreed with him that he was a lucky man to have been invited by the bouncing, big-bosomed cheerleaders to walk onto the field and feel their zucchinis. Such an honor must have made him feel good.

"No, it was not good," he replied, annoyed by my response. "You know there aren't any real women in a television set, just glass and a picture tube, so it feels cold."

"Not very satisfying?" I asked, veering sharply to keep in step with his feelings but pleased to have him pop into my world.

"Well . . . I could hold out my hand and feel their zucchinis." And here he left my world as suddenly as he had entered it and traveled back in his "photographic imagination" to the brilliant football field where dancing rows of cheerleaders leapt and spread their legs in obvious invitation. "But," he murmured, now deep within his dream, "they all put ice cubes in their underpants."

I did not have to be outsmarted by Mr. Nouvelle too many more times before I dropped the interpretation of his delusions as a primary goal. For one thing, interpretation had connotations of accuracy that I found uncomfortable. For another, it didn't work. Even when I felt quite sure I had touched on the real significance of Coke, for example, Mr. Nouvelle would rearrange his world just enough to prove me wrong. He drove me to conclude that delusions cannot function as a protective shield unless they remain impenetrable. So I substituted participation as my objective, and without quite realizing it became more interested in the transactions that went on between speaker and listener—such as being shut out or being asked to applaud—than in correct interpretation.

Also, participation did a better job of explaining the curious excitement I felt when captured by some intricate tale of an arboreal society, for instance, where mothers had enormous compound eyes like those of bees. How completely I became involved then. With the usual tools of understanding rendered useless, or at least insufficient, I was thrown back on childhood memories of enchantment. There seemed no choice but to yield to magic. Thus, as Mr. Nouvelle began a story, leaning across the table and fixing me with his hazel eyes, I became his accomplice, his cameraman. As he directed, I created pictures of watchful, buzzing mothers who shed their shells on the trunks of trees like locusts. On cue, I turned the enormous, newly hatched insects into nuns at his parochial school. I made roses grow from the ends of their fingers. I watched them walk into their students' dreams on a beam of light.

As we sat there in the meeting room, often inadvertently matching each other's gestures—a lean for a lean, a grimace for a grimace—there was nothing we could not imagine. There were no realities, however distant, we could not juxtapose. And in some wonderful way the Mr. Nouvelles on the ward knew instantly that they had captured me and that, like Scheherazade's King Shahriyar, I wanted them to live to tell the rest of their stories.

Indeed, I always wanted to hear more, for these webs of delusions had a haunting quality about them that I did not encounter in any straightforward retelling of a life. Mr. Nouvelle's dinosaurs, for example, whether adrift in an empty summer meadow or moving like shadows through a snowstorm, always seemed to stand for more than themselves. And so did his miraculous transactions—be it the provision of soda and cigarette butts for the dinosaurs or the removal of parts of his brain by the enemy. Whenever he spoke he alluded to the power of love to keep the mind together and the power of misunderstanding to break it down. It seemed to me that in every one of his stories his two-edged imagination took on the towering forces of disorder. The Dinosaur Man indeed belonged to an endangered species, and his life seemed to depend on keeping just one good story ahead of his own disintegration.

Of course, my interest in these legends put the storyteller in a peculiar and unexpected position. Ms. Goldman's generosity was not overlooked, and Mr. Nouvelle found that his lurid sexual fantasies did not elicit the accustomed response, namely that it is wrong for you to ask for love. Instead, these men and women were taken seriously, and their stories, far from being a waste of the therapist's time, as some believed, became the occasions for our most successful duets. It did not matter in the slightest whether the tales were "true" or even comprehensible. As soon as they expressed a willingness to speak and I an eagerness to listen, a connection was made and a second story begun. At first, this subplot was largely mute and, for me, consisted of listening and of echoing what I guessed were the important phrases.

"She was trying to kill me when I have no 'glose' by being blown up on Krypton Blood which came from me in a big explosion, maybe eight septillion megatons on Krypton and to hell with me to the end. Also I have no soul, so it must have popped out of me," said a patient who surrounded himself for hours at a time with an all-but-impenetrable barrier of words.

"She was trying to kill you?" I'd interject when he took a breath. Or, "You have no soul?"

Gradually, however, patients like Mr. Nouvelle would begin to answer or elaborate. After several months some permitted a still more expansive exchange. Cautiously, they inched away from the protective solitude of their impermeable imaginations.

"And then," I was able to say to Mr. Nouvelle on one occasion, as our exchanges broadened, "and then we will start a garden just below the farm pond where the land rises toward the forest. We will plant some bean seeds when the earth is warm and see what happens."

Slowly Mr. Nouvelle agreed to become part of this new story, which told of two people rambling through sun and shade in a land where neither could understand much of anything and certainly could not see into the future. For short periods of time he agreed to participate in this shared story that we commonly call living, and, like all good stories, it proceeded from day to day with the same basic question.

"When the beans grow and need something to climb on, what will we do then?" Mr. Nouvelle asked, as we strolled up the hill under the early-summer sun.

"Build a tepee with poles," I replied.

"And then?" he asked in a voice that did not remind me of a dinosaur's. "And then?"

What's Going On in There?

This person who was in my brain this week—raising hell in my brain—makes it very difficult for me. People bang on my head trying to get out.

PATIENT on 9-2-D

The dopamine hypothesis . . . states that there is a hyperactivity of dopaminergic systems in schizophrenia.

HAROLD KAPLAN and BENJAMIN SADOCK,
Synopsis of Psychiatry

For years I did not think to ask delusional patients what was wrong. With outpatients, "What's wrong?" was my first question, but on Ward 9-2-D I turned to the first page of each bulging chart and read off the names of their problems—"schizophrenia, paranoid type," "bipolar disorder, mixed" (manic depression), "major depression, recurrent," and so forth. And I believed that in those names was contained an explanation of what had gone wrong and a guide to the treatment that would hopefully make it right. Of course, each individual who now made his home on the second floor of Building 9 had unraveled in a unique way—pushed beyond his ability to cope by all manner of accidents, injuries, and betrayals—but when it came to the truest and most helpful explanation of his distress, I turned to the currently popular medical model of mental illness.

In simplest terms this model assumes that many of the major mental illnesses come from a genetic predisposition which under certain circumstances develops into a neurochemical abnormality. The result, a brain that doesn't work right; the cure, a chemical that restores normal functioning. Unfortunately, this scenario rarely plays itself out so straightforwardly. For some patients, medications seem to restore thinking completely. For most, the changes produced are of a more ambiguous nature, and for a sizable minority, drugs do nothing more than subdue their feelings and help them sleep. Members of this last group make up the bulk of the population on back wards.

Regardless of the limited effectiveness of antidepressants, lithium, and antipsychotic medication in restoring the patients on 9-2-D, no one seriously questioned the medical model or suggested that its truly breathtaking biochemical insights needed to be augmented in any major way. For example, during grand rounds—a weekly meeting in which each patient was interviewed individually by a team of specialists including a psychiatrist, social worker, nurse, therapist, and others—we all assumed that an imbalance of chemical messengers (neurotransmitters) was the proximal cause of the illness and that the mental confusion this imbalance created made it difficult for patients to learn to live among other people.

All our observations fit this framework. Whether the dietician reported that Mr. Nouvelle had lost twelve pounds or the occupational therapist reported that Ms. Goldman's conversations were becoming so loud that no one could concentrate on braiding belts, we all spoke in terms that could be explained by unbalanced chemicals and modified by a change in medicine and a boost in social savvy. In fact, so wholeheartedly had this medical model of mental illness—with or without its addendum of social rehabilitation—been embraced at Mountain Valley and elsewhere, that alternate explanations—such as terrible mothers, the devil, and masturbation—had been left behind. With them had gone such old practices as long-term therapy, exorcism, and farm labor.

But among the patients themselves, alternate explanations survived.

"I was hazed so bad in military school that I had to be institutionalized," I heard a man say in the dayroom.

"My mother put *ooo*'s and *aaa*'s in all her words until it was impossible to stand up to her," said another in the smoky canteen. "I am still afraid of these savage words."

"I would have no troubles if I could return to earth and live alone there," said a man with beautiful slanted eyes and a deep distrust of "you humans."

Abuse, sin, invasion, magic—gradually I learned that to ask for a patient's story or even to ask honestly for an account of his day was to be given a host of explanations. All but the most withdrawn advanced some theory that purported to explain how they came to be residing at Mountain Valley, apart from the familiar settings and people they had earlier known. Often these explanations were illogical and dramatic. Always they implied the kind of help that the patient believed he needed. Soon I routinely asked every patient I dealt with, "What went wrong?"

One of the first things that struck me was how varied the patients' explanations were and how consistently they differed from the theories held by experts. Only one patient spoke of neurotransmitters. The majority found it both intellectually difficult and morally distasteful to see their problems in terms of neurochemical aberrations and social backwardness. Perhaps, I thought, they objected to the medical model's assumption that madness is one of the body's problems, which has little to do with the person himself, or perhaps they disliked the social rehabilitators' idea that they should try harder to behave like the rest of us. In any case, after listening to explanations for several months, I found myself with two questions. First, were some explanations more fashionable among patients than others, because they either made better sense of their experience or were more comfortable to live with?

And second, did it matter that staff and patients held such apparently divergent views of mental illness? Did it matter that the stories I heard in the basement canteen about "what's going on in there" were so very different from those written in the charts?

Among the more fashionable explanations of mental illness held by the patients on 9-2-D were those positing a physical problem, although these reasons were rarely used alone. Like everyone else, patients are affected by the times in which they live, and both on and off the wards the explanations I heard reflected a more medically oriented and a more mechanistic way of thinking than I had found in earlier accounts of insanity.* Whereas the Romantic poet William Blake claimed madness is a creative state of artistic frenzy, for example, the imagination unleashed, the 300-pound outpatient Baby Joe claimed that his "flusterated and dizzified" mind had simply run out of gas. "Why cain't they jes fix it by pourin' in them li'l pink peels?"

Two other patients I knew argued that dirt and germs were being sucked into their systems. Another believed he had gotten syphilis when a dog breathed on his sandwich. Still others thought they had bees or machinery in their heads. And in a single breath the Dinosaur Man invoked a physical cause—and every other kind of reason—when he explained that "my eyes are confusing me and I don't know why an ophthalmologist doesn't fix them unless he thinks that I've killed people and that I believe I'm better than he is so he won't fix it so that my eyes won't bring things in wrong and put stoppages on the murdered mind."

Although bizarre, these medical and mechanical explanations of mental illness were in tune with the prevailing ideas of the day. Patients like Baby Joe and the doctors who treated them waited together for the silver bullet.

But, as I said, patients rarely used physical explanations alone.

---

*Histories of madness have been written from a number of different perspectives including the insane themselves, D. A. Peterson, ed., *A Mad People's History of Madness* (Pittsburgh: University of Pittsburgh Press, 1982); psychiatrists, see G. Zilboorg, *A History of Medical Psychology* (New York: W. W. Norton, 1941); and social historians, for example R. Porter, *A Social History of Madness* (New York: E. P. Dutton, 1989).

More prevalent were explanations that put into quasi-scientific terms what appeared to be a combination of social, psychological, and biological causes of distress. Many schizophrenics, for example, complained that their minds had been taken over by powerful forces, such as gravity coils, the Central Intelligence Agency, or drugs, and that this intimate invasion had compromised their memories in one or more essential ways. Thus robbed of a unified identity, they found it impossible to understand themselves or to communicate their plight to others.

Lloyd Bartlett used this reasoning with an interesting twist. He believed that his problems stemmed more from a superabundance of mental ability than from a lack or disorganization. I first met Mr. Bartlett, a thin and unusually white-skinned man of about fifty, in a transition group for outpatients who had recently been discharged from the hospital. Even as he walked into the clinic's meeting room, almost hiding behind the other patients and dressed as unobtrusively as possible, his vigilance singled him out. Like a scout in enemy territory, he seemed bent on sizing up the terrain and making a quick assessment of each person present. As the other men and women ambled in and sat down, his gray eyes flickered over all of us. He had an intense, rather sardonic gaze and, according to the voluminous chart that chronicled his hospitalizations, his intelligence was even more powerful than his glance.

Mr. Bartlett was also aloof. Every week, as six or eight of his peers settled into the easy chairs that clustered around a low table in the center of the room, he would select the chair nearest the door. There he would sit, very still, observing. He did not want to *be* observed, however, and when he intercepted my frankly curious glances, he gave me the feeling that I had trespassed against him. Gradually I learned that he did not want me to read in his face or posture messages that might appear there against his will or, worse still, might arrive from a part of his personality that he himself had lost track of. When I spoke with him, I felt I was conversing with a double agent who could not quite remember which alias he was using.

Indeed, over the next several months Mr. Bartlett gave me two accounts of his life. One was unremarkable.

"I was born in a small town. No big deal," he said with a shrug, and his tone made me suspect that he had long been at odds with the ordinary. He had attended public school, he went on to say, and had fought with his older sister, who was "superior in all ways" and was, of course, the family's favorite. It was Mr. Bartlett, however, who went to college and majored in anthropology. Some ten years later he moved to Michigan to take a position at a university museum, and there, among the cases and cabinets of Algonquian relics, he began having trouble. His memory of those early years was hazy now, he admitted, but he believed that a turning point came when a woman he had been dating for several years left him. "I became depressed," he recounted, in his characteristically spare manner. "I was hospitalized. The rest of my life? Similar disappointments."

The account of Mr. Bartlett's other life was vastly more exciting, yet curiously bereft of details.

"Much has happened, and the memories are so vivid," he would begin, sitting straight in his chair and fixing his eyes on some distant point behind me. "Once I was dropped on the Mendenhall Glacier in Alaska. I was nine." As usual, his precise story got right to the point. "I was dressed in a special fur, but I had no food and no map. . . ." And again, as usual, the story faltered just as it was about to take flight.

"Well, to make a long story short, I was rescued."

"How? By whom?"

Mr. Bartlett frowned in annoyance. "Oh, it has a downward turn."

"Meaning?"

"Meaning it has no meaning. They say it never happened."

Many of Mr. Bartlett's stories were frustratingly amputated in this way, and it became clear that he had begun questioning the validity of this other life and the usefulness of talking about it. This put him in a painful position. To be understood, he needed to tell me his story. To be respected, he felt he needed to hide the parts that were delusional. Certainly the staff in a dozen hospitals had supported this second course of action, and I had to agree that learning to hide delusions is a useful lesson for anyone hoping to live outside the hospital. But this was not the only reason for Mr. Bartlett's reluctance to speak of his "other life." I began to notice that this other life rudely took over any conversation that centered on Mr. Bartlett himself. When this happened, he would fall into an angry silence, as if embarrassed by his loss of self-control.

In spite of his quandary, Mr. Bartlett gradually gave me an outline of this alternate life, which, although it lacked embellishment, contained a thoughtful explanation of mental illness.

"When I was six months old I began to walk and run," he told me, pointedly avoiding my gaze. "I could climb trees too and my mother would try to get me down. She couldn't.

"At seven months I was talking, but when I began to read—I used to drag books along behind me on my blanket—my father decided to destroy me."

According to this version of Mr. Bartlett's life, his father became convinced that Lloyd was not his child and began to plot his demise. At the same time, his older sister and her friends became jealous of his abilities. They called him Little Lloyd Fauntleroy and told everyone that he was strange. No school would accept the precocious toddler, and his mother could not handle him at home. In a desperate move, Mrs. Bartlett sent her son away in the company of an Indian who agreed to protect him.

"For two and a half years I lived in a basket strapped to the back of Bobby Two-ton Eagle," Mr. Bartlett stated flatly.

"Yes?"

"Well, I needed the protection," he continued, jumping over a hundred details that I wanted him to provide. "Benny Eiso, alias Medicine Man, wanted to test my resourcefulness because he didn't believe the reports given to him by the minister of Indian affairs, Armand LaCherry—about my walking and talking. So he would drop me on a glacier or in the wilderness to see if I could find my way back. Of course Bobby Two-ton Eagle tried to protect me," he continued wearily, as if he had gone over and over these accounts, "but when he was recalled by the minister—he did secret work for him—then Medicine Man could get me."

I was especially intrigued by Bobby Two-ton Eagle (also referred to as "the man who could not fly"), and gradually I gathered that he was a large, somewhat overweight Indian with black hair that sprouted from his head like a fountain of wet ostrich feathers. With his sharp black eyes and great beak of a nose, he could find food, spot danger, and pick out the faintest trail toward home. I also realized—suddenly—that I, not Mr. Bartlett, was supplying all the illustrations for these fabulously complex stories, and I had to be careful not to change the sense of his skeletal tales by fleshing them out.

One afternoon, for example, Mr. Bartlett told me that when he had been captured by Medicine Man, Bobby Two-ton Eagle had tried to reach him by constructing a bridge of vines over a chasm. Medicine Man had anticipated his move, however, and had sprayed all the vines with a chemical that weakened them. Bobby would have lost his life except that he had taken the precaution of sewing the leaves of the vines together into a parachute, which opened as he fell. Bobby then climbed from the chasm using thorns from a bush strapped to his feet, only to be bombarded with mutilated deer which Medicine Man catapulted from trees.

The action was characteristically complex. It had a dozen twists and turns, but *nothing* was described. In spite of myself, I provided a leafy jungle, dark, shaggy vines, and the bloody carcasses of deer hurtling from the treetops and thumping onto the trail below. In his "scheme of the world," Mr. Bartlett provided only ideas. His story was not a fable or a dream. It was more like a life-size model of an airplane constructed entirely of toothpicks. The trickier it became, the more Mr. Bartlett seemed to be building himself into a cage that separated him from the rest of the world, and, indeed, one of his major themes was a double dissociation, from himself and from others.

"When Bobby Two-ton Eagle did his secret work," Mr. Bartlett explained, "he blew the smoke of a special weed up my nose so that I'd forget things. I'd wake up and something would happen.

Then, blank, I'd go to sleep. Then I'd wake up and something else would happen."

"Does your memory still work like that?" I asked, intrigued by the mention of this common complaint.

"Sometimes," he replied after a pause. "I think the drugs they give you in the hospital damage your mind."

"How can you tell?"

"Because I often feel I'm in the world but not part of the world," he said quietly. "I'm a sleepwalker in my own bad dream of the world."

As often happened, Mr. Bartlett then moved from his discussion of medications back to the potions used by Medicine Man or Bobby Two-ton Eagle. His guardian's objective in knocking him out, he told me, was to protect him from the dangers of knowing too much and of becoming too attached to his keeper. He learned from Bobby that "the world is full of parasites who want what you know. The more you know, the more they try and get you."

Unfortunately, neither the induced amnesias nor the drugs in the hospital stopped Mr. Bartlett from thinking and imagining too much, and it was this great fund of vivid experience that made him the target of men like Medicine Man. When the latter wasn't trying to kill the clever Mr. Bartlett or experiment on his brain, he was stealing his ideas, especially his inventions for preserving dead raccoons.

"I had to develop special ways of thinking to stay alive," Mr. Bartlett once said, inadvertently hinting at the needs of a lonely and unhappy boy. "My mind had to become sharper and quicker just to keep ahead of Medicine Man.

"And even when I'm not in danger," he added thoughtfully, "I still think like that."

"Is that a useful habit?" I asked.

"It could be . . . , sometimes," he replied. "You're not bored that way, but people don't understand you."

As Mr. Bartlett grew older, the scene changed but the theme remained the same. He felt that he continued to work for people who stole his ideas and resented his intelligence. Simultaneously he was hounded by Medicine Man, who had discovered a new way of testing his ingenuity, namely hospitalization. Thus, from age thirty to fifty Lloyd Bartlett was hospitalized some dozen times. Each time it was a mutual declaration of war, and now it was clear that the prize to be won or lost was his "real" identity, his life. On one side, Mr. Bartlett and Bobby Two-ton Eagle struggled to hold on to the life they had lived or at least so strenuously imagined. On the other side, he maintained, dull doctors, aided by an even duller bunch of nurses and counselors, sought to stamp out his genius with mind-altering drugs. The staff seemed bent on demonstrating that the life he thought he had lived had never occurred. They urged him to believe that they had a clearer idea of his life than he himself.

"They used the phrases 'that is not true' and 'that never happened' interchangeably," Mr. Bartlett pointed out, with an astuteness not generally found on or off the ward. "Because our accounts don't agree, I don't exist."

"Do you mean," I asked, "that it is as if you had spent your life watching movies, only to be told that, since they were not true, you had not experienced anything at all?"

"Not exactly," he countered firmly, and I was sorry that I had compared the one life he had so obviously poured his heart into to so mundane an activity as watching movies.

One afternoon Mr. Bartlett sat in my office and tried to explain how these alternate accounts of his life—his own and the doctors'—came into being and how demoralizing the conflict between them was for him.

"When I was forty-five," he began, "I spent several months in Maine. I met this guide up there, a really superior man, I thought, who led me to the best trout streams. He reminded me a little of Bobby.

"It was this time of year," he continued, nodding toward the open window through which we both could see young leaves rocking on a warm breeze. "We fished a lot. Bobby Two-ton Eagle had taught me to catch trout with my hands, and I was quick. Every day I caught my limit, and on the last day—it's so vivid—I was standing right over the rapids when . . . this huge fish . . ."

The fair-skinned Mr. Bartlett sat straight and expressionless in his wooden chair, but for a moment he could not continue. "He pulled me in. I wouldn't let go," he finally said, jumping ahead as usual and leaving me to fill in the details.

Apparently there had been a struggle or perhaps an accident. In Mr. Bartlett's mind, the incident ended with his victorious landing of an enormous brook trout followed by its theft by the guide. The latter supposedly sold it to the local tackle shop, and a week later an outraged Mr. Bartlett found it hanging on the wall. He demanded the trophy, and when the owner did not comply, he tried to rip it from the wall. His next memory was of looking out through a hospital window.

"My memories of the fish became dreamlike and quite re-markably distant then. I got bored," he continued, probably de-scribing the effects of the antipsychotic medication he was given.

"Sometimes whole pieces of my past broke off like that."

Relieved of his delusions, Mr. Bartlett found himself with two springtimes to fit into the story of his forty-fifth year. One, he recalled, was full of the excitement of fishing and of a "powerful motivation."

"The other springtime was a degrading account of a middle-aged man," he said bluntly, "a man who let his imagination run away with him while he wandered *alone* through the Maine woods."

This "real" account suggested that all the cleverness, quick-ness, and ingenuity he prided himself on had never existed. It asserted that *nothing* had happened. "How am I supposed to fit 'nothing' into my life?" he asked angrily, shooting me a bitter look. "And what am I supposed to do with all the other things that happened to me? I have been threatened and harassed more than any man you know, and through it all I have consistently made the choices of a fair and self-reliant man." He scowled at the floor. "Is there no significance to that? No honor?"

A breeze stirred the curtains, and the perforated shadows of lace swayed across the bare floor that lay between us.

"I wake up now with sadness," he continued, lowering his voice. "I am tired of being so completely misunderstood."

I sat silently with this anguished sleepwalker and drew together what he had told me of mental illness, or "mental divergence," as he preferred to call it. He seemed to be telling me that he had come into the world with too much imagination and drive and that his constant need to fly while others walked aroused in almost everyone he met some form of fear or anger. Whenever these people could manage, they used drugs or some kind of power to break off pieces of his past and fragment his identity. In response, he built and rebuilt himself in ever more complicated ways.

In its essentials, Mr. Bartlett's explanation was echoed by several other schizophrenics I encountered, and I suspected that these men and women were experiencing a more or less common series of disruptions. They too had vivid cerebral adventures, which felt to them like excess brain power, and they too suffered the horrible "disconnections" which some associated with medication.

Unfortunately, clinicians cannot yet explain these sensations in a way that is both scientifically and emotionally sound. They cannot tell us, for example, what accidents of fortune cause the misfiring of neurons or deterioration of tissue that in turn cause the disconnections in memory. Although they know that the schizophrenic brain suffers from diffuse impairment and that its blood flow, balance of chemicals, and ratio of open spaces to tissue all tend to deviate from those of ordinary brains, the specific cause of the schizophrenic's symptoms has not yet been identified. Even the "fact" that schizophrenics have an overactive dopamine system, which is deduced from their response to drugs that are known to block the action of this neurotransmitter, may be questioned, since delusional patients with other illnesses that do not involve dopamine also show improvement with these drugs. In short, scientists cannot yet provide explanations, as they have in other areas, that make sense to the patients.

As common as the explanations were on 9-2-D that invoked mysterious medications and failing memories, they were outnumbered by speculations of a more purely social nature. These explanations asserted that illness is a punishment, either a just retribution for a crime that has been committed or an unjust consequence of an innocent misunderstanding.

Concerning the first, the chaplain at Mountain Valley told me that fewer and fewer patients came to him convinced they were being punished for heinous sins. Nevertheless, he and I both encountered a few men whose voices told them they had transgressed. One explained to me that he had been sentenced to seventeen years of suffering for a crime he could not remember—"but it musta been bad." What his doctors called schizophrenia was, in his word, "purgatory." The voices in his head were less intense now, he said. "They whisper to me that the sentence is nearing the end."

Others expressed similar convictions, and occasionally I could glimpse a possible reason for their belief, as in a patient whose failure to watch her sister had resulted in the child's being run over. Most suffered silently beneath their guilt, however engendered, but a few, such as Matt Franklin with his pressured brain, suffered publicly for all of us at Mountain Valley. Gliding down the corridors, his gaze fixed rigidly on some distant point in the universe, this self-appointed sacrificial lamb would bless passersby with a practiced hand. With his pain he believed that he bought us moments of "bliss and joy." (His blessings were unreliable, however, and once, as he slid by, hand upraised, he said, "Good morning, Octavia. You look wonderful. My condolences.")

In any case, Mr. Franklin was a man who had found a sense of purpose in his illness, and, although I did not see him often, he seemed to me to move through the days and months with greater equanimity than some.

I had expected to discover that certain explanations of mental illness were more comforting than others, but it increasingly became apparent that *any* well-wrought explanation brought with it a welcome sense of predictability. Even if the patient's reasoning were completely wrong by conventional standards, he gained the comfort of thinking that he knew what lay both ahead and behind. Only those without any explanation at all or those for whom the reasons for their suffering shifted like glass in a kaleidoscope seemed entirely adrift.

The complement of the idea that the mentally ill are sinners is that they are victims. They are suffering because they have been misunderstood and mistreated. As a cause of madness, this one-two punch of misunderstanding and mistreatment has been advanced at least since the eighteenth century, when the practice of institutionalizing the insane was begun. The essence of the argument was (and still is) that the patient was first misunderstood by his family, usually as he tried to march to a very different drum, then placed in the care of people who abused him. The first of these insults sent him over the edge, the second kept him there. "To have been so loved, or so duped by the appearance of my family's love, and to be so abandoned," wrote John Perceval in *A Narrative of the Treatment Received by a Gentleman, During a State of Mental Derangement*, which he published in two volumes in 1838 and 1840.

But this was just the beginning. Although Perceval, the son of the then deceased prime minister Spencer Perceval, attributed his derangement to an excessive preoccupation with religion exacerbated by an unsympathetic family, he was certain that his troubles were worsened and prolonged by the treatment he received in Dr. Edward Long Fox's private lunatic asylum. He claimed that the care he received at Dr. Fox's perfectly confirmed the very fears that insanity had set upon his mind. He arrived worried that he was a bad person, and indeed he was treated as one "incapable of desire as well as of judgement" who deserved no more consideration than "a piece of furniture." He also entertained the delusion that he was a being controlled by voices he was utterly powerless to resist. Again, his treatment suggested that this was exactly the case. He was controlled by staff and had no say in any aspect of his care.

> Men acted as though my body, soul and spirit were fairly given
> up to their control. . . . I was never told, such and such things
> we are going to do; we think it advisable to administer such

and such medicine, in this or that manner; I was never asked, Do you want anything? do you wish for, prefer anything? have you any objection to this or to that?

In short, he felt treated like a child or an imbecile. And what kind of improvement, he asked testily, did the doctors believe that this high-handed formula would produce?

Shut him up from six A.M. to eight P.M. regardless of his former habits, in a room full of strangers, ranting, noisy, quarrelsome, revolting madmen; give him no tonic medicines, no peculiar treatment or attention . . . , debar him from all conversation with his superiors, all communication with his friends, all insight into their motives, every impression of sane and well-behaved society! Surprise him on all occasions, never leave harassing him night or day, or at meals; whether you bleed him to death or cut his hair, show the same utter contempt for his will or inclination; do all in your power to crush every germ of self-respect that may yet remain or rise up in his bosom . . . , and give him no opportunity of retirement or self-reflection; and what are you to expect? And whose agents are you; those of God or of Satan? And what good can you reasonably dare to expect? And whose profit is really intended?

Few patients at Mountain Valley Hospital were as articulate as John Perceval, and none had cause to complain of physical abuse. Nevertheless, like him, many ascribed the continuation of their troubles to a frustrating inability to make their desires—and, more important, their worth—clear to their protectors.

When I met Maurice Nouvelle, the Dinosaur Man, he was, by all accounts, an expert patient. He had lived on almost every ward in the hospital and had lived through many changes in policy and administration. He had been given all the major psychiatric medications and a course or two of shock treatments. He had been left alone, talked to, tested, and, most recently, rehabilitated within a biopsychosocial framework. For all this care he was by turns grateful and furious.

One rainy afternoon I joined this slight, bespectacled man in the corner of the dayroom and asked him to describe the care he had received over the years. As usual, he had been leaning forward in one of the big, brown chairs as if watching something, and I had pulled another chair into his line of sight and positioned myself between him and his visions. I wanted to know if the hospital felt different to him now than it had, say, fifteen or twenty years before.

After a few confusing turns around the issue of whether he should be mothered like a boy or treated like a man—a concern that I, too, puzzled over—he gave me some specifics. First on his list of complaints was the inability of most staff members to speak English.

"They sound like chipmunks," he confided. "I can't make out a word, but the nurses say *I* talk ragtime and they won't make their panties invisible. A sophisticated man has a doctoreate . . ."

"What would you say to the nurses if they could understand you?" I asked quickly, hoping to deflect him for a moment from his sexual concerns. "What do they need to know to help you?"

"Cherish and care," he answered after a pause. "A good squaw makes feeding mean caring correctly . . . nourishing food . . . , being looked up to . . . , and helps you fix something. She gives you Coke and cigarettes and makes her panties invisible."

Mr. Nouvelle went on to tell me that the good moments in his life were few and far between. They came roughly every hundred thousand years, when "the little women" cherished him for the qualities that made him a sophisticated man, his "articulate wisdom," "ethereal imagination," "charm," and, of course, his "thirty-eight good dicks." His bad days were far more frequent, and on these he suffered doubly, once because the girls didn't love him and again because they were so insensitive to his torment.

"They think we're in ecstasy when we're really in agony," he complained, his voice rising. He began to rock slightly and paw the floor.

"How long would they last if they knew what *really* went on in your head?" I mused aloud, but received no reply.

"So when will they fix me?"

"I believe they are trying."

"Noooo!" he groaned, slumping still farther forward. "I mean why don't they give me the right medicine? They must have a reason! Am I too good? Do they think I've—"

"Mr. Nouvelle," I interjected firmly, "they don't have a medicine for every one of your problems."

"*Of course they do!*" he roared and threw himself onto the floor in a heap.

As often happened when stung by a fact, Mr. Nouvelle retreated into one of his rituals. Still sitting on the floor, he began kissing the ends of his fingers—little finger to thumb and back again. Gradually he calmed himself down.

Although Mr. Nouvelle's explanation of why he remained institutionalized was laced with fantastical metaphors, it was remarkably accurate. He realized that he was not deeply understood—not his language, not his suffering, and not his apparently presumptuous desire to be loved and cared for. Nor was he "looked up to" for any reason. Nor was he given effective medication in spite of the best intentions. In short, he was not getting the psychological understanding, the social acceptance, or the biological treatment that he felt he needed.

Here was a problem. Here was a significant mismatch between what was being asked for by the patients and given by the staff, and in large part it grew from the different explanations that each group gave of mental illness and the treatments these explanations implied. Mr. Nouvelle, Mr. Bartlett, and others who explained mental illness as a troubled part of living—but living nonetheless—seemed to be saying, "Help us think straight if you can, but in any case understand us and value us for who we are right now." On the other hand, the staff, favoring the idea that mental illness is a series of mistakes in need of fixing, agreed with the use of medication but offered acceptance and release only in exchange for acting normal. This placed both patients and staff in a difficult position.

For the patient, the staff's efforts to get him to "act normal" required that he start a war between his thinking and his behavior. Only if he could successfully override his characteristic ways of thinking and become a credible impostor could he leave the hospital and live among ordinary people. For the staff, the mismatch between what they offered and what was needed resulted in misunderstanding and often in a sense of futility. Some said they felt squeezed between the enormous needs of the patients and the modest resources of the hospital. Others implied that they were trapped between a personal belief that the chronically mentally ill would never recover and their role as agents of recovery. And, more poignant still, many acted as if caught between the need to provide good treatment, which involved careful listening, and the need to survive as an employee, year after year, which required that the deepest pain and anger be excluded by a selective, and soon habitual, deafness. It sounded to me as if the patients' most basic problems—those that rumbled far beneath all particular imbalances—were too costly to address.

"You've done very well this week," said the ward psychologist to a patient during rounds, as eight or ten of us sat around the coffee-stained table in the old meeting room. "You've followed all the rules."

"Hey," added a social worker with good humor, "stick to sports and weather, skip the sex talk, and you'll sound like one of us."

Fresh from a session with Mr. Nouvelle, fresh from his descriptions of green beans singing on the vine, "motes" drifting through his mind, and Leonardo da Vinci producing an alternate set of anatomical drawings—"You know, he could have used a chicken"—I was taken aback by these attempts at reform.

"But wait," I wanted to say, "do you really want to replace Mr. Franklin's belief that he has the power to bestow great gifts with better hygiene? Exchange Mr. Bartlett's labyrinthian plots for better eye contact? And trade the Dinosaur Man's rich and haunted imagination for . . . for what? And what do you imagine you would have left?" I continued, beginning to sound like the aggrieved John Perceval. "And whose agent are you . . . ? And what good can you reasonably dare to expect?' "

Given the modest position that I held in the hospital at that time, it was not my place to rearrange a philosophy that worked subtle compromises among more needs and desires than I could even name. So in my mind I left that long, coffee-stained table then, with its charts and litter of pencils, and returned to sessions I'd had in this same meeting room with my patients.

I remembered the time that Mr. Nouvelle and I had begun to mimic each other's speech and gestures and the sensation we had, amid our high laughter, of filling this dusty room with flashes and bursts and fountains of light. I remembered sitting with Dallas Grey and listening to his curious account of a world war as fought by first-graders during a thunderstorm. I remembered Mr. Clauson's terror when green plums grew in his ears and Mr. Franklin's apocryphal memories of sin and the gifts of "flowing green light" that he gave in order to be forgiven. "They tell me that all my thinking has been wrong," Lloyd Bartlett had once told me in obvious distress. "What am I supposed to do with that? If everything I have ever done is a delusion, what is left? I am so tired of being asked to throw myself away."

Rounds went on around me. Dental work was prescribed for this one, new glasses for that one. Patients were praised for acting normal, which, I readily admitted, might be the one ticket they would ever have to a life outside the hospital. For the most part the patients half-listened to the sounds the staff made, and in their turn the busy doctors talked above what might have been the sound of singing.

Over the intervening years, I have come to few conclusions concerning the moral treatment of the profoundly mentally ill. I am still not entirely clear about how one's explanation of madness affects or should affect its treatment. I still do not know how medications may best be used, or whether behavior modification, with its goal of social adjustment rather than the patient's well-being, is ever really in the best interests of the delusional patient. But I do believe that the medical model of mental illness excludes too much of the patient. Using this model, only parts of the patient are considered, and even when these parts are assembled by a multidisciplinary team into a manikin of a schizophrenic or of a manic-depressive, the spirit that animates the real person gets lost. Especially in chronic cases where mental illness and the desperately clever adaptations it inspires have become central to an individual's personality, the patient's own story and explanations—his delusions and his imaginary worlds—must be included.

Indeed, I believe that the patient's story must form the context within which treatment begins. In these chronic cases, as with the more familiar neurotic, the moving experience of being heard and believed is required. For me, the essence of healing is the rare combination of being understood, as perhaps the somewhat perverse or unusual person you are right now, and loved. Who among us, Mr. Bartlett, would not have someone catch the sound of our soul singing as it did before it lost its courage and its love?

Keep Me Connected to God

*Schizophrenia is the ultimate and most paradoxically absurd . . .
defense, beyond which magic defenses can go no further. . . . [It
is] the denial of being, as a means of preserving being. . . . He is
dead, in order to remain alive.*

R. D. LAING, *The Divided Self*

As Laing observed thirty years ago, some schizophrenics have
an unnerving way of acting dead. They do not speak when
they are spoken to. They lie motionless on the floor. They try to
walk through chairs. They seem insensitive to heat and cold.
Above all, many on the back wards seem either entirely disconnected from other people or related to them only in the most
temporary and superficial ways.

"You're not my real mother," I overheard Mr. Mountbank
say to his real mother when she came to visit him on the ward. "My
real mother has a brown reindeer and lives in California." This tall
and stunningly handsome man listened to his mother in silence for
ten minutes, then added, "I was born to a mouse and moved to
a queen." With that, this platinum-haired young man rose from

the table in the small dining hall on 9-2-D and strode off down the corridor with a graceful urgency that I associated more with a tennis player than with a mental patient.

Clearly, I was not going to learn anything about the social ties of schizophrenics from the isolated Mr. Mountbank, I thought after watching this exchange, and I tentatively assumed that he was one of those "dead" or walled-off patients who had no connections at all.

A slim and well-coordinated man in his early thirties, Mr. Mountbank had been hospitalized for more than a decade. During this time, he had maintained a profound silence, which he broke only rarely with utterly crazy talk. Dressed in a faded Mexican wedding shirt, the significance of which I never learned, he paced the corridors, ate his meals, attended activities such as arts and crafts, but almost never spoke. One of the other patients on the ward believed him to be the statue of an angel. And indeed he might as well have been for all the notice he took of others, his family included.

Then one day I saw Mr. Mountbank escorted onto the ward at a time when he would usually be someplace else. A physician I didn't know was waiting for him in the dayroom. He asked Mr. Mountbank to be seated. The latter gave no indication that he had heard him.

"I am sorry to have to tell you that your sister has died of cancer," said the doctor, looking steadily up at Mr. Mountbank, searching for the first signs of his reaction. There was none. "Cancer of the breast," he added.

Still no reaction.

"Cancer that then spread to—"

"Spaghetti," Mr. Mountbank interrupted, looking blankly at the physician. "She died of eating spaghetti and noodles, and I feel responsible for not stopping her."

That curious statement was all there was to Mr. Mountbank's reaction, except that when it was time to go to arts and crafts, Mr. Mountbank refused, thereby neglecting to finish his paint-by-number version of the Last Supper. Instead, he stood in the day-room . . . and screamed.

After Mr. Mountbank surprised the ward by expressing feelings that had been completely hidden for over ten years, I began looking for relationships among the patients, or between patients and outsiders, in a different way. There were two obvious questions I wanted to answer. First, to whom, if anyone, were the patients on 9-2-D connected? Second, were these "real" relationships, meaning like ours? Or did they proceed according to some different set of conventions? With Mr. Mountbank in mind, I suspected that direct questions would not get me far. Instead, I would have to look and listen in some odd as well as ordinary places.

The first thing I noticed was that on the ward nurses and cigarettes were the big prizes. Both drew patients like magnets. Although psychiatrists had far more power over important decisions, like the selection of medication and the possibility of release, they did not interact closely with the patients except, of course, for the legendary Dr. Sweetheart. Usually it was the male and female nurses and aides who saw the patients every day, who fed, washed, praised, and punished them, and who became—reluctantly—a kind of family for them.

The "house" that this family lived in revealed a lot about how the relationships were supposed to proceed. Like many other wards, 9-2-D was laid out in the shape of a thin H. Connecting the sides of the H was the nurses' station, the center of power and activity. It was there, behind reinforced glass, that the nurses and aides answered the phone, wrote in the patients' charts, dispensed medications, and drank coffee. It was a dark room, having no outside windows, and it never had enough chairs for the crowd that liked to gather there at the beginning of each shift.

Especially at eight in the morning, when the psychologists, psychiatrists, and social workers came on the ward, the nurses' station was the center of activity. Two or three nurses sat at a table piled with clipboards, dividing the tasks of the day. Which aides would escort the patients to activities? Were extra meals needed for patients too agitated to leave the ward? Was anyone needed for

"one-on-one," meaning was there a patient who seemed so determined to hurt himself or others that he required constant watching? Similarly, was anyone needed to watch "the quiet room,"
where an assaultive patient might be lying in four-point restraints,
on his back on a cot with wrists and ankles fastened to the bed
frame with leather cuffs? As lists were drawn up and calls made to
other parts of the hospital, the ward psychiatrist and psychologist
were likely to pass through, either to check on the general condition of the patients or to see that medications and group therapy
sessions were in order. In the midst of all this coming and going,
an unbelievable amount of coffee was drunk, and, on good days,
we ate day-old crullers from an enormous grease-stained carton
that the night shift had left on the table next to the coffee machine.

We were a self-contained bunch in our crowded little fort. We
had our own food, a lavatory, a chart room, an office, telephones,
and, at the center, a small but complete pharmacy. From the
nurses' station we could see along both corridors and into the
dayroom. Of course, *in* the nurses' station we could be watched like
fish in a tank by the patients.

"Mary Frances! Mrs. Quinette!" shouted a patient through
the glass, pulling his T-shirt higher up his chest and rubbing his
belly.

"Mr. Whitman, don't—"

"They found the baby in my stomach, on the X ray."

"Mr. Whitman," repeated the nurse, who was also this patient's advocate or case manager, "don't yell through the glass.
Knock on the—"

"They took an X ray and saw the baby with a snake in it. That
proves I'm a woman," and with that the volatile Mr. Whitman
disappeared around the corner and into the men's room.

"Mumma," mumbled another, his face pressed like an old
pancake against the glass.

"Gentlemen, get away from the nursing station," Mary
Frances said loudly, and for a few minutes the tide receded.

As the layout of the ward made clear, the staff had more
protection and more power than the patients. The former led from

a unified position of strength, the latter followed helter-skelter. This held true for their relationships as well, and the kind of connection that most members of the staff wished to establish was that of the efficient caretaker guiding the compliant patient. Nurses and aides kept patients healthy, clean, and on their feet, and although many of the patients grumbled that they had "no rights," at some level most realized that this was an essential form of care and a kind of comfort as well.

In spite of the limitations that efficiency, emotional stability, and policy placed on the range of relationships possible between staff and patients, it seemed to me that some nurses chose to move cautiously toward what looked like a low-key kind of mothering. It was not unheard of, for example, for a nurse to get teary-eyed when a patient was transferred to another ward or released. There were also curiously close relationships between certain of the very assaultive patients and the one nurse or aide who could usually calm him or her down.

Then there was the matter of the gracious acceptance of compliments. There were always one or two particularly attractive nurses on 9-2-D, dark and sassy or blond and sweet, and often they developed dexterous ways of juggling a proposal of marriage or the offer of a ride in a Cadillac. To accept would be to dismiss the offer as ridiculous, to decline would be to wound in a more obvious manner. Instead, I overheard these nurses thanking their admirers for their compliments in a way that reminded me of a mother accepting dandelions. For a moment, at least, the patients' power to please was acknowledged. Given this subtle form of reward, several of the men on 9-2-D became positively courtly.

"We do *not* want to get married, Miss," said a scarecrow of a man whose imagination had been permanently captured by the South in the Civil War and who now suspected that he was "a lot like Robert E. Lee," "but when we get out, would you do us the honor of taking a tour in our five-thousand-three-hundred-and-twenty-six pound Pontiac Star Chief?"

"Billy Mark, you scoundrel," replied the head nurse with obvious pleasure. "Did you own a Pontiac Star Chief?"

"Ahh, Miss Hendrix, let me tell you about that car," he replied, and for the next two or three minutes he dreamed out loud of a former life and of a time when he was handsome, smart, and always dressed in white.

In addition to the exchanges that I could observe on the wards, I heard stories of relationships that sounded more like friendships than parent-child duets, although it was impossible to know how memory had changed them over the years. Dallas Grey remembered talking every day to his favorite nurse, Pookie Hauptmann, and Maurice Nouvelle dimly recalled an aide who had taken him out to dinner once a week "for a long, long time."

There were less exclusive "friendships" too, such as Jason Whitney Ill's complicitous association with the male aides, a relationship based on his vociferous belief that all males were geniuses and all females were birdbrains. "You have the brains of a peacock, Madame," he once said to me, "the brains of a teeny-weeny bird."

At the other extreme, there was at least one alarmingly intimate relationship maintained by a patient in Building 3 who was reported to have a nurse friend from another hospital who sidled up to his bedside to be tickled with feathers.

Among the patients themselves, however, neither caretaking nor befriending were prominent pastimes, and the connections I saw seemed semiconscious at best. After lunch, for example, it was common to see eight or ten men, all smoking, sitting around the periphery of the first-floor lounge. Most were silent, many rocked or tapped. Ivana Goldman negotiated a hot deal with invisible business partners, and an absolutely wild-eyed man, whom I'd seen when I first arrived on the back wards, inscribed enormous figures in the air and claimed to be reading Coptic braille. No one spoke to anyone, unless he wanted to cadge a cigarette, and if patients' paths crossed as they left the lounge, they ricocheted off each other like windup toys. Except for Mr. Brunetti and Jolinda Muniz, that improbable pair who had been sitting together on hospital benches for over fifteen years, there seemed no connections I would call friendships among the patients on 9-2-D.

When the more able of these patients took the bus to Hillsdale on Saturday or Sunday, however, it was a slightly different story. It was the chaplain who tipped me off and suggested I spend time at Edna's Donut spying on Tyler's Variety or vice versa.

Hillsdale is an old mill town that falters for two or three miles down a steep valley from the edge of the hospital grounds on the high end to a series of small ponds all named after minerals at the low end. Edna's place is near the hospital end of town. It looks like a sun porch attached to an old wooden house.

For several weekends I staked out Edna's. I had no problem spotting the patients, because, just as in therapy, they never took off, or even unzipped, their jackets. Having bought their cigarettes across the way at Tyler's, they wandered in after 9:00 A.M., ate silently, and didn't wipe the jelly off their mouths. After they'd eaten, they watched. Gradually I noticed that the special target of their attention was a group of men and women who carried in their eyes and in their posture much of the same wariness as the patients themselves.

"I'm watching you," said a swarthy patient to one of these outside people, who, I later learned, was a muskrat hunter on welfare.

"I'm watching *you,*" the latter replied.

Nothing much more than that happened at Edna's in the morning, when the Hillsdale folk were around, but in the afternoon, when business slowed, a kind of "open house," led largely by the townies, got under way. A woman who could receive cosmic ski reports from several planets, thanks to silicon chips that had been implanted under her scalp by the Central Intelligence Agency, took the first shift, and anyone who wanted to watch her—or talk with her—dropped into Edna's right after lunch. Later Arnold, an astrologer of sorts, took his turn, and around suppertime either the Monopoly Man or the jocular, 300-pound Baby Joe (who "din like no rang-rang, yak-yak bullshit, no doctors' I-don-know bullshit") was on hand.

It was a curious sensation to realize that under the ordinary goings-on of a small town there was an all-but-invisible group of people made up of the poor and the disabled who watched each other, occasionally befriended each other, and, I learned later, somewhat absentmindedly exploited each other both financially and sexually. They sat in coffee shops. They walked along sidewalks. They looked straight ahead so intently that they deflected the gaze of passersby.

Apparently the price of admission to this group was need and the silent acceptance of each other's peculiarities. The acceptance part of this bargain was rarely managed by the most withdrawn of the hospitalized patients, especially when they were dealing with others like themselves. But when one member of a potential twosome had a little energy and resilience, a relationship of sorts seemed possible. I remembered reading that the best predictor of a patient's success in remaining out of the hospital is the number and quality of social contacts established in the community. I could count the number, but an assessment of the quality was harder to come by.

Nevertheless, I had learned something that I could bring back to Mountain Valley. The glue that lightly bonded the relationships I'd observed at Edna's seemed to be mutual acceptance and the recognition of each other's usefulness or purpose in the world. This second quality reminded me of the nurses' acknowledgment of a patient's power to please or, in the language of the outside community, acknowledgment of the intrinsic usefulness of relaying ski reports or catching muskrats. Being of value seemed to underlie the connections made among mental patients, and later, when I had the ski-report woman in therapy, she ascribed to her acquaintances qualities such as humor and reasonableness that few others would have recognized. Of course, she knew a "nut" when she saw one, but this label did not top her hierarchy of attributes. It did not invalidate every other quality the person possessed.

Now who in the hospital, I wondered, would accept patients without trying to change them and would also see them as people with a use and a purpose in life? Who wanted a roomful of sharply silent watchmen or a shuffling line of magpies? Again the answer came from the chaplain. It was God.

" 'God created you,' I tell them. 'God loves you. You serve a purpose for Him.' "

As I sat in a plain office with this small, gray-haired man, soft rock playing quietly on his radio, the chaplain went on to tell me that it was not difficult to spot the Lord's presence in Mountain Valley. Many of the patients, he said, had at least a rough idea of what God saw in them and what He wanted from them. They especially took His requests seriously. With this I agreed but, human nature being what it is, I had expected to find that on 9-2-D God's requests would be astutely tailored to the resources of the patients. I had expected Him to ask a fat man to eat and a space alien to fly. This, however, was not at all the case.

"Father," I interjected, "I agree that the Lord always asks a patient for an important gift—not something trivial like making your bed or saying please—but why does He seem to be telling one patient to suffer for seventeen years, another to die in agony, and a third to swallow a set of keys?"

" 'You *thought* you were hearing God's voice,' I told that unfortunate man," explained the chaplain, who had, himself, found this particular patient lying prostrate in front of the altar with a very sore throat, " 'but God wouldn't punish you that way. We punish ourselves.' "

"That was three years ago," the priest continued, leaning back in his desk chair. "The patient was taken to the hospital, and the keys were removed. Of course he still hears God's voice, only now it tells him to stop smoking."

The chaplain drifted on soothingly, like his music, and I gathered that the key-swallowing patient had "a good relationship with God." The patient tried hard not to smoke and was proud when he succeeded. He lay on the chapel floor every day and got "inward peace." He said that memories of his mother and father came back to him then. He remembered a happy childhood.

"And what about the patients' relationship to you?" I asked of this black-clad priest who had served in hospitals for several decades.

"Oh, as chaplains I think we are very fortunate," he replied, "more fortunate than the medical staff in that respect."

"Meaning you have a closer relationship to the patients?"

"Well . . . , perhaps. The patients are like children for the doctors—for the team—but they are more like brothers and sisters to us. They're just another person."

The chaplain went on to surmise that the patients at Mountain Valley felt most comfortable in the company of chaplains, aides, and janitors. "These are the people who let them talk without stopping them all the time. We're also the ones who are least likely to keep them waiting."

"True, but do patients see you as a powerful source of help? As equal to a doctor?"

"Not usually," the chaplain answered easily. "We live near the bottom of the ladder. But I have told doctors to wait on occasion," he continued, referring again to that ubiquitous sign of professional status, "and so have the patients. For some of them spiritual healing is almost as important as physical healing."

The chaplain then told me about the couples he had married, the violent patients he had calmed, and the overly zealous he had tempered.

"I've had to take the Bible away from some patients. They start preaching in the dayroom and making all sorts of crazy interpretations. I find it best to steer them toward the Psalms."

"Do you know Mr. Nouvelle?" I asked, thinking of crazy interpretations.

"Of course." The chaplain chuckled. "He's the one who looks through the religious pamphlets, then asks me where I've put the girlie magazines. He knows the prayers in French, you know. I hear him when I am preparing the Mass."

"And what do you think Mr. Nouvelle wants from God?"

"He is suffering like the rest because he doesn't have a loving relationship," he answered obliquely.

"Does he know what God wants from him in exchange?"

"Ask him," suggested the chaplain.

I did not fool myself into thinking that it would be easy to ascertain the nature of the relationship that Mr. Nouvelle believed he had with God, but a week or so later we inadvertently touched on the topic of religion. It was a hot afternoon, and the dogwood trees along the hospital road stood motionless in the summer heat. Mr. Nouvelle and I had started off for our garden at the edge of the hospital grounds when a black man crossed our path.

"Do you see me as brown or white?" Mr. Nouvelle asked.

"White," I replied. "Well, actually both. Your face and hands are tan and your chest is white."

"How do *you* know what color my chest is?" he retorted, laughing at my preposterous assumption of magical powers.

"Because I can see it when your buttons come undone," I replied, and I pointed to just such a gap within which swung a small cross and two medals.

Mr. Nouvelle looked down at his half-open shirt. As we approached the garden, he said, "I think you should know something about medals."

And thus, as we sat in the checkered shade of a small pear tree, I was introduced to the patron saint of mental patients.

"St. Dymphna, pray for me," I dutifully read on the tin medal he pulled from his shirt. "Who is St. *Dime*—?"

"*Dimf-na,*" he corrected. "St.-Dymphna-virgin-and-martyr, St.-Dymphna-consoler-of-the-afflicted, St.-Dymphna-friend-of-the-helpless, have mercy on us. . . ."

Returning after a time from the chapel in his mind, Mr. Nouvelle told me the story of St. Dymphna. He got most of it wrong. In fact, I learned that St. Dymphna lived in the sixth century, first in Ireland and later in the village of Gheel in Belgium, where her miracles and cures are still celebrated. When Dymphna was not much more than a child, her mother died and her father decided to marry his daughter, for none as fair or gentle was to be found in all the land. Appalled, Dymphna fled to Belgium. Her father followed, confronted her, and in a fit of insane rage beheaded her.

Only gradually did the residents of Gheel realize how precious were the memories and remains of Dymphna, but in the thirteenth century they erected a church in her name. Miracles and cures began to occur, and St. Dymphna's fame as the patroness of the mentally disturbed changed the village to quite an astonishing degree. At first, patients traveling to her shrine were housed in an annex of the church, but as their numbers grew, they were taken into ordinary homes as guests. Later still, the Infirmary of St. Elizabeth was established to care for the most acutely ill. Still St. Dymphna's fame grew, and it became common knowledge throughout Europe that hopeless patients often returned to a nearly normal life in Gheel. There evolved what we would now call a foster-care program that has had no equal anywhere, and only in the last ten years or so have St. Dymphna's charges begun to feel less welcome, as Gheel becomes more modern.

Mr. Nouvelle said that praying to St. Dymphna might make you feel better. Remembering Edna's, I thought that the people of Gheel might give you the chance to rattle around town and report on cosmic ski conditions or sell muskrat pelts. In either case, the point was well made. Both God and the people of Gheel seemed to offer not only what patients sought from the staff at Mountain Valley—namely comfort for the body—but also what a few sought and obtained in the community—acceptance and a recognition of their usefulness.

A few days later Mr. Nouvelle returned to the ward for his noon medications and invited me to attend Mass. Still thinking about Gheel and St. Dymphna, I readily accepted. With perhaps six or eight other patients, we walked down the hill and entered the chapel. It was a simple room designed to be used by all denominations. Modern stained-glass windows carrying no design more complicated than a dove or an outstretched hand marched along the walls, and at the front of the church was an altar and, behind that, a tan curtain.

Wheelchair patients from the hospital's medical ward were moving to the front as Mr. Nouvelle and I walked in, and two patients were already sleeping in the pews across the aisle. A beeper went off behind us. As the man in the row ahead stood on his seat to see who was being "beeped away," I could see that he was wearing the most enormous religious medal I had ever seen. A young priest walked solemnly down the aisle, and the room quieted. I whispered to the Dinosaur Man that I would follow his lead and do whatever he did.

"Didn't I bring you up right?" he shot back, referring to his belief that I was his dinosaur daughter. How could I be ignorant of the service he attended one way or another every day of his life?

The Mass got under way and audibly gained momentum as the patients intoned the familiar prayers. The congregation rose. We slumped forward over the next pew. The congregation sat. We knelt.

"Pssst, the curtain," a patient hissed, and another quickly walked behind the altar to draw back the curtain, revealing a life-size cutout of Christ, who seemed to be flying at us through the air.

After a short sermon on the wisdom of talking to others, a prayer was said which ended with the priest's words, "and the peace of Christ be with you."

To my astonishment, we leapt into action. A deaf man in the front row shot down the aisle shouting, "Peace of Christ! Peace of Christ!" and high-fiving everyone he could reach. Electric wheelchairs began buzzing in circles like beetles on their backs. The pious gentleman in front of us who had been mimicking each of the priest's broad gestures leaned so far into our pew that I thought he would fall over. I shook everyone's hand—in front, behind, to each side—and I saw all around me an earnest and active goodwill that I had never witnessed before in Mountain Valley. Could it be that a connection to God best enabled these "dinosaurs" and "space aliens" to relate to each other in a somewhat realistic and comforting way? Already starting to build a theory on this singular observation, I turned to Mr. Nouvelle.

"The peace of Christ be with you too," I said, smiling warmly. He drew back, looked at me blankly, then pitched himself headlong into my stomach. I fell backward onto the narrow pew, my breath and my ideas about God knocked out together.

A few minutes later, as we were trudging back up the hill, Mr. Nouvelle asked me if we had "done it" in the chapel.

"No," I responded somewhat testily. "I don't think God wants you to 'do it' in the chapel."

"Who told you that?" he asked with annoyance, then drifted off into his own thoughts, as he often did. Suddenly he turned to me with a look of pure terror in his eyes.

"They queered my photographic imagination so I can't see the nuns anymore in St. Anne's," he said with great agitation, holding out his thin arms. "They put me in chains. My arms and legs. No," he corrected himself, "I mean they gave me something heavy to carry."

Mr. Nouvelle staggered across my path as if burdened with a great weight. "I can't carry anything!" he shouted angrily. "They don't understand. Is it too fragile? Too heavy? I drop everything. I do everything wrong." His arms collapsed against his sides. "My thoughts won't stay down where they belong. I'm going to throw up."

As Mr. Nouvelle doubled over in angry despair, there came to my mind other times I had watched him "die in agony." I had thought then that he was reacting to a loss of something or someone at Mountain Valley, but now I believed that he was suffering from a more cruelly pervasive disconnection.

Much later that summer evening—far from Hillsdale and Mountain Valley—I returned in my mind to the alarming problems of disconnection. Although I had seen Mr. Nouvelle get disconnected before and had watched other patients succumb to "the rage" or "the sickness" or "the nightmare," I was never prepared for the look of betrayal I thought I saw in their eyes. Nor did I become accustomed to the devastation that followed the rupture of what naively might be called only a superficial or a delusional relationship. A picture came into my mind at that moment of Mr. Nouvelle huddled in the corner of the dayroom looking extremely upset. Although almost too distraught to speak, he had finally blurted out that the Father had died again. Missing too was the image of the Blessed Mother which he always, *always* carried in his head.

"Are they dead forever?" he had asked, and I was struck, as

I had been before, with the beauty and directness of that question. His eyes told me that he was as disoriented as he was distressed by his losses, and indeed he seemed to have slipped his moorings, fallen apart. He lay in pieces on the chair in front of me. He did not look as if he could put himself back together, much less reassemble the memories of those he had apparently lost.

So here were the complements to my questions concerning connections. I had discovered that all but the most withdrawn patients on the back wards did, in fact, make a modest number of connections. Not all these relationships were like ours. They were not as well integrated into the rest of their lives, not as realistic, probably not as satisfactory; nevertheless, patients did connect. They built relationships with themselves, with God, with pals, and most managed to construct some sort of "family" on the ward as well. But then came the disconnections, and these were as numerous and varied as the connections themselves. Rotations ended. Doctors moved. Patients left. Sisters died. And every one of these disconnections rocked the patients' world.

Who knows what thoughts went through their minds then or in the months and years that followed? Perhaps they forgot as much as they could, choosing to circumscribe their disappointments within as small a circle of time as possible. Perhaps they froze whatever memories were left into a monument, an unalterable symbol for "family" or "doctor." Some, however, struggled to keep the severed connections alive in whatever bizarre way they could. Dallas Grey, for example, fashioned the memories he retained of the fantastic Dr. Sweetheart into a crazy story that kept him company as he wandered between the ward and the greenhouse on those days when he remembered he had a job. Even Dallas Grey, whose badly fractured memories ran to blood and torture, told himself that Dr. Sweetheart still stood atop Building 2, reminding him "like a father and a son" to take his medications. For Mr. Grey, Dr. Sweetheart was not—at least he was not always—dead forever.

These were the sad, ordinary partings that went on every day somewhere in Mountain Valley. But what about patients like Mr.

Nouvelle, whose disconnections exceeded in intensity and extent those experienced by all but the least fortunate of human beings? What did they do when psychotic storms descended as unseasonably as death itself and all their connections went down together?

I think now that this is probably the most awful aspect of mental illness, these catastrophic disconnections when the self betrays itself and disappears with no promise of return. I try not to imagine that recurring form of death. I try not to imagine the stone-deep pain of those multiple bereavements.

As with ordinary losses, so with this deepest of confusions and despairs. Some patients seem to jettison as much of their identity as they can manage. Others appear to freeze themselves and their worlds into delusions that roil and rocket through realms of torturous fantasy yet never really move. And some reach out to reconnect for a minute or an hour time after time after time. Perhaps these last are the ones who offer their suffering as a gift to God. Perhaps that is all they have. And maybe there is some obscure and courageous usefulness in what they do.

It is a mystery to me why Mr. Nouvelle has never given up. I cannot imagine what gives him the strength to pull the treacherously unreliable memories he has of himself as a dinosaur or as God the Father together into some semblance of a soul that manages to go on living. Perhaps it is a monstrous lust which keeps him forever yearning to dive into that most intimate of connections and drown himself a thousand times in a sea of naked women. And perhaps it is his faith.

One afternoon, at the time of our regular Wednesday meetings, I could not find Mr. Nouvelle. He was not poking around for cigarette butts in the Annex, the chapel basement, or any of his usual hiding places, and I could not imagine where he could be. I stood uncertainly at the entrance to the dayroom, listening to the sounds of the coffee maker being refilled and the janitor squeaking down the hall with his cleaning cart. The afternoon sunlight came in through the dayroom windows and lay across the floor in great bars that almost reached the open entrance to the men's room, and, as I looked in that direction, I heard a low, mumbling drone.

Walking to the open archway, I looked in along the row of sinks and steel mirrors that lined the wall. There, standing before one of the mirrors, was Mr. Nouvelle saying the Mass. As usual, he was dressed in his homemade uniform with the magic symbols scribbled on the shoulders of his blue shirt and a tie tack holding down a dirty, red tie. Standing alone in that wide, white room of tiles, he looked as if made of some lighter and less flexible material than flesh.

"In nomine Patris, et Filii, et Spiritus sanctus," he said to the mirror, crossing himself several times. Abruptly, he leaned anxiously toward his own reflection.

"I will always pray," I can still hear him saying urgently. "But I still get disconnected from the Father. Pray for me," he implores. "Keep me connected to God."

IN THE CLINIC

Learning to Lose in the No-Win Situation

Wanda McGowan was seventy years old when I first heard her screeching at her husband, Willis, on the second floor of a local hospital. Huddled under a purple-and-yellow afghan that she had insisted on bringing to the hospital with her, this small, bespectacled fury was doing her best to exact from her husband—and from everyone within earshot—the same reluctant obedience she enjoyed at home. Admitted for the treatment of varicose veins in legs that even nurses who didn't like her agreed were exceptional, she had been sobbing and complaining constantly. But not merely sobbing and complaining. Wanda, I was to learn, had an inimitable way of combining desperation with theatrics to produce chaos. So in need of help did she appear, so cleverly did she interleaf gratitude, tears, and irritation, and so unerringly did she divine the one personal weakness in each of her well-intentioned caretakers, that all who came in contact with her found themselves sucked into the vortex of her perpetual confusion.

"She's done it again," a nurse told me breathlessly as I

emerged from the hospital's annoyingly silent and unhurried elevator. "We're all yelling at each other, I can't tell whether she's dying or laughing at me, and now some man is on a camping trip in her room!"

The situation was indeed out of hand. For reasons that remained obscure, Wanda's husband, Willis, had moved in with bag lunches and a folding campstool, which he set up at the foot of her bed. There he sat night and day, peering up at the television set across the room. Or rather, there he sat until fatigue overcame him every several hours and he fell with a crash to the floor. The patient in the bed next to Wanda's had finally lodged a complaint, in writing, against Willis. Wanda had pleaded loudly for Christian compassion, but when Willis offered to let himself be dragged from the room, she threw an unbelievable fit. As I arrived in Room 202, the nurses were struggling to restore order.

"Hello, Mrs. McGowan, I'm—"

"Doctor! Oh, dear Doctor. Thank God you're here. Listen, I am not afraid to die. I've lived a good life. I have two adorable children—twins. Do you know Lester and Lorrie McGowan? She was married, of course, and still uses Blackman, dreary name."

"Mrs. McGowan, I'm not a—"

"Wil-lis!" she suddenly shrieked. "I'm going and you aren't at my side!"

Wanda grasped her throat, threw herself back on her bed, and began to make a horrible gargling sound in the back of her throat. She was doing "it" again. I commanded her husband to leave the room.

"Close the door!" snapped Wanda in her turn. To my astonishment, she sat up, readjusted her heavy glasses, and smiled.

"Willis is such a baby," she sighed, addressing me now with complete composure. "But I have him this time. Come sit on the bed, right here, and I'll explain why he doesn't *dare* leave the hospital now."

Twenty minutes later I emerged from Wanda's room—when she said I could go—feeling that I had been outmaneuvered in every way possible. This woman beat me at tricks I thought I was good at and she beat me at games I didn't even know I was playing. She was a professional.

During Wanda's stay in the hospital, neither the nurses nor I ever managed to quell the turmoil in Room 202, and by the time this voracious woman was released, I was so annoyed by my own impotence that I had agreed to make weekly home visits. I had three or four strategies I was aching to try.

And so, at the beginning of my career, I happily stomped onto the McGowan battlefield and learned to lose. It was a wonderful introduction to the conundrums that I encountered at Mountain Valley and elsewhere, and that seem to arise wherever the peculiar art of therapy is practiced. For example, whose agent was I? It was not Wanda herself who had asked for my ministrations. Dual requests had slid under my door from the patient's family and from "society," if the staff in a hospital can be said to represent the communal will. And what were these requests? Was I to help Wanda feel better? Was I to support her desire to change the way she thought or behaved? Or had I been called in to make life easier for those who lived around her?

None of these questions had yet occurred to me as I drove out of town to McGowan's Pine Cliff Rest. The couple owned eight log cabins, which they rented out, and as I moved up the driveway through the pines, I could see what I imagined were their own living quarters perched above the motel's office. I parked beneath a line of tall firs before noticing that there were small wooden markers indicating the correct spot for each of some dozen vehicles. I could see Wanda's fifteen-year-old Ford pulled up to a marker that read OWNER and Willis's truck next to a smaller sign that read TRUCK. I backed out of SNOWDROP and found VISITOR.

"Yoo-hoo, Doctor!" called Wanda from a third-floor window.

"Hello, Mrs. McGowan. You know I'm not a—"

"Be a dear and use the side door. Willis will let you in, and just leave your shoes on the landing."

The window closed with a bang. I made my way to the side of the house, where a door opened into a narrow hallway.

KEEP DOOR SHUT read a sign tacked to the outer screen door.

TURN OFF LIGHT read another in the hall itself.

I climbed two steep and poorly lit flights of stairs and, reminded by another sign, was just taking off my shoes when Willis emerged.

"Come on in," he said cordially. "It's nice of you to visit old folks like us. Wan has been having a terrible time of it, *and*," he continued, lowering his voice, "she's been complainin' like—"

"Wil-lis!" screeched Wanda. "Willis, don't say stupid things. Do you think the doctor has time to waste? She's here on business, bizz-ness. Go mind yours." And with that the five-foot-tall Wanda all but shoved the bear-size Willis out the door and down the stairs. "Garage!" she shouted after him.

Looking around, I found myself in a large country kitchen with a truly amazing assortment of antiquated appliances. There was a coal cookstove, right up there on the third floor, a wringer washer, and a peculiar assortment of grinders and mixers clamped to a long counter. Wanda ushered me into her parlor and instructed me to admire her African violets. I was also given a chance to exclaim over family pictures (I noted Willis was missing) and a postcard collection of the fronts of churches. I was told where to sit.

"How's it going?" I finally asked, when she had settled her smartly dressed self into a chair opposite me and propped her bandaged leg on an ottoman.

"Just fine!" she said with alarming intensity. "Willis has spoiled me, and the neighbors . . . , well . . . I didn't know I was so popular."

There was an awkward silence.

"Ahh, that's good news," I said. "You've managed to stay off your feet and keep your leg—?"

"Oh my no," she broke in. "I can't trust Willis with the cooking, of course, and he's as dangerous with a vacuum cleaner as he is with a car. But I manage. Always have. Always had to."

Tears sprang out of nowhere into Wanda's eyes.

"You've had some hard times?" I questioned sympathetically.

"I could write a book," said Wanda, leaning back in her old

velvet chair and dabbing her eyes with the handkerchief she kept tucked in the cuff of her blouse. "And no one would believe what I've been through. . . . My mother named me Lester before I was born, you know. She and my father wanted a boy so bad. But there I was, a little mite." Her voice began to break. "A little . . . innocent . . . baby."

Drawing out the words, Wanda transported herself to the depths of despair in a matter of seconds. I hustled to select one of my *ultra* sympathetic questions and was just leaning forward earnestly when she squealed with laughter, poked me with her cane, and limped off to the kitchen.

"Sit right where you are," she called back. "I have a surprise."

Wanda reappeared several minutes later with a tray of food.

"You need to gain some weight," she said, with a wink I could not interpret, "and everyone *loves* my roll-ups."

"No, thank you, I've just eaten," I said, not catching on to rule number one in the McGowan household, namely that innocent Wanda was boss.

"Wash your hands and use the pink towel," she directed, setting the food on the table, and, although I am not pleased to admit it now, I walked into her bathroom and read six more notes.

I ate. She talked. I offered sympathy. She turned it aside. I began to feel irrelevant and a little stupid. She reeled back my attention by crying at her own descriptions of deprivation. Willis stayed in the garage.

An hour later, I bid Wanda good-bye, and in parting set down some rules of my own. I would see her every Wednesday but only for an hour, and no food. She laughed.

"Give me a call before you come," she called gaily from her window as I climbed into my car. I was catching on. I didn't even try to answer.

Over the next several months, Wanda and Willis gave me as brilliant a performance of marital discord and mutual manipulation as I have ever witnessed. And I was not merely an onlooker. I got hands-on training. On the second visit, for example, the table was set for two and the food already served. I demurred. Wanda immediately complained that her eyes were bothering her and she would have to go to bed. She "forgot" the third visit and was not at home when I called, but a week later she teased me about the wonderful treat she had in store for me. By this time I'd begun paying attention to my instincts. I was on full alert. The treat was not food, however, but a photograph album in which she kept photos of, and postcards from, her former nurses and therapists. They loved her so much, she told me. And they were so beautiful. Hard to believe, but they ended up telling her their problems. I had decided beforehand to smile for the whole hour. My face hurt.

Just as I was getting used to being punished for not eating, but before I began to wonder if Wanda's shenanigans meant she didn't want therapy, she called in great distress. I was to come right away. No, she could not discuss it on the phone, but suffice it to say that Willis had left her. Agreeing to advance her regular appointment by a day for such a catastrophic event, I arrived and was greeted by a now annoyingly composed Wanda. Soon she was weeping, however, as she told me of Willis's murderous plan to make her suffer. The day before, she had twisted the ankle of her better foot, and the doctor who treated her, knowing she lived on the third floor, called the town's rescue service to take her home and carry her upstairs.

"Of course I wouldn't let them," she explained breezily. "Our insurance only pays part of the cost."

Thanking the doctor, Wanda had hobbled stoically from the office. Once in the waiting room, however, she began to moan and insisted that Willis carry her piggyback to the truck. All went well until he clumsily hit her bad leg against the door. Naturally she had begun "sobbing to break your heart." With every one of her sobs, she explained (and every one of his steps), she slipped lower on her husband's bony back until right in front of the truck, right within reach of affordable transportation, that "cagey old fool" had stumbled to his knees.

"God damn it, Wanda, shut up and get off me!" he had roared.

Of course she collapsed on the pavement. Willis shoveled her into the truck and, to her horror, drove straight to the hospital. There he checked himself in with a hernia and left her to take an ambulance home.

"Right this minute," concluded Wanda through a sheet of tears, "he is flirting with the same nurses who took such poor care of me a month ago."

Silly me, I thought, using one of Wanda's favorite expressions. For a minute I had supposed that the stumble and the strain were accidents. Actually, Wanda knew what she was talking about. Within the year Willis managed to throw himself from a ladder each time Wanda thought she had him trapped into caring for her. He even got back into the hospital the following winter by having an accident while riding one of those big adult tricycles with the Day-Glo flags on the back. He ended up on the hood of a car. It was parked.

The squabble over who gave care and who received it seemed fairly easy to understand. Apparently, Wanda wanted Willis to grow up and start taking care of her for a change, especially since varicose veins and eye problems (a detached retina) were eroding some of her natural ebullience. By everyone's account, she had always worn the pants in the family, and now she wanted Willis to take over—a little. Yet when Willis began to act on his own, there was trouble. He joined a local scavengers' club whose members all had metal detectors and a passion for getting something for nothing. They gathered every Monday morning to look for whatever might have dropped into the sand and pine needles along Silver Pond or under the bleachers at the high school football field. Willis was a natural for this activity, and within a month he had completely outfitted himself with a short plastic rake, a sifter, spaghetti tongs, and a carpenter's apron, all of which he hung around his middle. He even had a wonderful cap with a transparent green visor, which made him look like a park ranger.

"From Mars," snapped Wanda, who was extremely annoyed by the entire enterprise. At first she claimed to be embarrassed by her husband's fondness for "droppings." Next she said she needed his help on Monday mornings, when the group met, but at last she addressed the real issue. She composed a personal ad listing all Willis's "real" traits and threatened to run it in the Date Maker section of a local "swap 'n' trade" paper.

"No woman of any age or any means would have him," she declared with bravado, and I began to understand that her husband was caught in a no-win situation. "I need you to grow up and take care of me," Wanda seemed to be saying to him and, at the same time, "I need you to remain a baby so you won't grow up and leave me." For a time this made me feel sorry for Willis, a response, I soon learned, that he enjoyed enormously. It also made me wonder if everyone who came in contact with Wanda got caught in some kind of double bind.

Willis's uncanny ability to hurt himself whenever Wanda was disabled eventually gave me the opportunity of meeting Lorrie and Lester and of seeing how they coped with their mother. By this time I had learned from Wanda that the twins were "a mistake." Willis was Wanda's second husband, and she had told him the day they married, and many times afterward, that she was not going to have his children. She was thirty-five at the time and past "the hard years." He was twenty-seven and "still a baby." In any case, they married and, prompted by a real-estate ad, moved to the country. There they bought the motel with eight log cabins. Willis was supposed to furnish and repair them. She would manage the renting and the finances. The two worked like slaves for nearly three years, Wanda told me, until she discovered she was pregnant.

"It was a disaster! Our plans, our whole life . . . out the window. But you know me, I got down on my knees and prayed. 'Dear Jesus, let this be the best little baby in the world. Let him never cry so that his mummy can work and work and work.'"

Of course, Wanda was violently upset when she learned she was carrying twins, but Jesus, who answers the prayers of the innocent, gave her the two best children in the world.

Lester was very bright, very handsome, very successful—very much like Wanda—and was married to a hateful woman who thought she was better than anyone. Nevertheless, Lester was a darling and always called Wanda his girl or Miss Lovely Legs.

Unfortunately, Lester lived some 6,000 miles away in Hawaii and could not express his affection as often or as directly as he wished. Wanda simpered whenever she spoke of Lester, and the one time I saw them together, she hung on his arm and was more coquettish than I had thought possible at seventy.

From what I could gather, Lorrie was different, or perhaps, being a woman and geographically closer, she had a different selection of strategies to choose from for getting along with her mother. She lived nearby and was frequently present on Wednesday afternoons when I made my visits. However, I cannot say that I ever really met her. Lorrie would greet me on the third-floor landing, then disappear down the steps I had just ascended. She would pick up a newspaper as if to clear a space for us to sit, then disappear for the rest of the hour. I would see her coming down the hall and be halfway through the word *hello* when she would vanish into a closet. Of course, she saved the really good tricks for her mother, like going for a glass of water and never coming back.

"Mrs. McGowan, excuse me, but did you notice that the glass of water you asked for half an hour ago hasn't appeared?"

"But I'm not thirsty anymore," Wanda replied, somewhat puzzled by my concern.

"That's not the point. I thought that—"

"Lorrie is a good girl," said Wanda, charging to the defense of her thirty-something-old daughter, then swerving onto a different tack. "The truth is I didn't have the time for her when she was a baby. Two was too much for me."

Gradually I noticed that Wanda's relationships with her children were not all that different from the one she and Willis had negotiated. To Lester she seemed to be saying, "Fuss over me the way your father never has. Let my wishes be your commands, but for goodness' sake don't let that wife of yours push you around." In fact, so upset did Wanda become in the presence of Lester's allegedly assertive wife that the couple no longer visited. Lester came east alone every couple of years to show "his girl" a good time, and Wanda occasionally flew to Hawaii to give her daughter-in-law a lesson in falling short. These visits were brief, however, because Wanda was unable to tolerate for more than three days at a time the idea that Lester's wife had a sizable say in how the couple lived. Once, when Wanda stayed an entire week, she became so frustrated with her lack of control that she offered to buy back Lester's allegiance with savings bonds.

Not surprisingly, Wanda's underlying directives to Lester concerning dependence and independence emerged in ways that made compliance impossible. As with Willis, if Lester did not follow her orders, Wanda believed he did not love her and would not take good care of her, but if son or husband did follow orders, they showed themselves to be henpecked fools. No one ever knew just which of the two commands—"follow my orders" or "stand up for yourself"—was being given or followed, and one of the more poignant consequences was that on the rare occasions when anyone in the McGowan family expressed affection, no one could tell whether the expression sprang from ingrained obedience or a spasm of free will.

With Lorrie, the question of whether she was or was not inextricably attached to her mother was worked out in a somewhat different way. Wanda had a fantasy that the two were confidantes, yet she repeatedly made it clear that if any of Lorrie's thoughts were unbecoming to a Christian, they were unwelcome to her ears. That Lorrie had a great many unbecoming thoughts I could only guess from Wanda's habit of mobilizing an overpowering innocence when a hurtful topic was broached.

"She sleeps now in the arms of Jesus," she told me when I asked if Lorrie's boyfriends concerned her. "God has always kept me pure and innocent," she added, and I had long since learned that a reference to innocence meant that Wanda had just had the last word.

In spite of the storm of mixed messages that constantly swept through McGowan territory, not to mention the verbal warning signs that kept so many topics out of bounds, Wanda gradually told me something of her past. Born into a poor family with three boys under the age of two—her mother had also had twins—Wanda felt she had inconvenienced everyone. She could not be dressed in the same hand-me-downs or housed in the same large dormitory as her brothers, and the special considerations that had to be made for her were not easily affordable. Wanda's main memory of her father was that when she was fourteen he said she was growing up too fast. Shortly afterward he took a job haying in another town and never returned. There were rumors that he had taken up with another woman, others that he had moved to California alone. Wanda's mother kept the family together until her daughter was sixteen and shortly thereafter prayed to Jesus to marry her off.

"I was innocent as the morning," Wanda said, and I noticed that this phrase, in addition to identifying a topic as off-limits, flagged it as outside her control and responsibility. Wanda's first marriage was a complete disaster, and although she told me that she had come through it with her sweet and trusting nature still intact, the experience so confused her husband that the dreadful man never again bathed with hot water.

"Ahh, yes," I had learned to answer by this time. "The old hot-water trick."

In any case, after crying for three years, Wanda walked out, took a job, and saved her money. Some dozen years later she met Willis and saw in him a replacement for the tireless worker she herself had been. When they bought the motel with her savings, she figured that he could wash the walls and repaint the cabins. She herself would design the advertising and win the hearts of guests and townsfolk alike.

Wanda was not good at winning hearts, although I could never be sure whether or not she knew this. She had a "*dear* friend Dolly," but Dolly lived far away. There was a neighbor lady, but she was moody. The church women should have adored her, but instead they seemed subtly disappointed.

The word *but* figured prominently in all Wanda's accounts, and gave to her thinking as well as to her stories an up-and-down motion that induced a kind of mental motion sickness.

"I've *always* known I'm a remarkable woman," she once said, clapping her hands in girlish glee, but two minutes later she was nearly sobbing over her hardships.

"It's a real tragedy that I never received a college education," she said sadly, then jounced me over an emotional thank-you-ma'am by adding, "but really, I've accomplished a *great* deal without one. I would have made just the best history teacher. Don't you love to read about wars?" Here she giggled, clasping her hands again. "World War II was horrible! Just horrible. I pray to Jesus my Savior . . . ," and here her voice trailed off as if outstripped by her plunging imagination. "Oh those poor innocent children," she gasped, and again began to sob.

Very occasionally even Wanda herself wanted to get off this mental roller coaster, which seemed to rise and dive so dizzily through her thoughts that fears, disappointments, joy, remorse—everything was reduced to a blur. I remember when she first learned that her vision was deteriorating to the point where she would soon be legally blind. She sat in her velvet chair, framed with African violets, and admitted that she could not understand why she was so bossy with Willis. She argued the case with herself for a few minutes, then exclaimed in exasperation that she could not think straight anymore. "I'm tired of trying to get people to treat me right," she said, with more insight than I'd given her credit for. "I don't know what anybody wants."

Least of all yourself, I thought, and marveled at how difficult and often disagreeable it is to admit what you really want from another person. But throughout the time that I knew the mercurial Wanda, I did not think deeply enough about what she did *not* want from me.

I assumed I was a sounding board and a support for her—the meat and potatoes of therapy—and I assumed that she would feel better and be grateful for my efforts. Once or twice I even thought she might be interested in loosening her grip on her family or, as she put it, in relaxing her campaign for proper treatment. In other words, I assumed that I was working for Wanda even though I was also listening to family members who apparently wanted me to moderate her moods, and even though I was working for an agency that wanted to contain her escalating medical bills. (Wanda's emotional problems translated themselves so readily into physical ones that money could be saved by using a therapist to treat her disappointment rather than a physician to treat the pain and fatigue her emotions engendered.)

In spite of my belief that I was helping Wanda, I had more nearly allied myself with the McGowan family. Actually, I was even further off the mark than that, for I was working for what I thought this family *ought* to want. Of course, this put me in a whole series of no-win situations, the simplest being that if I tried to ameliorate the treasured family war I was a home wrecker, and if I went along with the status quo I was useless. Because I continued to focus only on the strategies used by the McGowans, however, it took a good long time before I saw that I, too, had let myself be trapped.

One of the more fascinating aspects of the strategies I was observing—each adopted to meet Wanda's contradictory demands—was that they revealed the needs of their organizers. Willis, for example, was still trying to beat Wanda at her own game. When she wanted him out of the house, he came in, and when she wanted him in, he went prospecting for coins. Neither won this contest of wills, but it bound them together tighter than vows. Wanda had the advantage of being the leader. She started things, and Willis responded predictably. Willis had the advantage of appearing blandly innocent. He got the sympathy. By contrast, both Lester and Lorrie tried to outflank the double binds. Neither was willing to pull out of the game entirely, Lorrie because she would not forgo the pleasures of paying her mother back by disappointing her and Lester because he still enjoyed the role of Mother's best and closest ally.

I also saw that Wanda herself had strategies for meeting her demands. "I am special and deserve special care," she sometimes seemed to be saying, yet most of her actions suggested that she believed the opposite. She considered herself an inconvenience, as perhaps her parents had done, and believed that only someone as immature and unsure of himself as Willis, as angry as Lorrie, or as much in need of praise as Lester would put up with her. She thus gave herself the impossible job of keeping them all insecure enough to be immobilized yet hopeful enough of finally getting the love and revenge they wanted to remain active players in the family drama. In addition, she needed to pretend that this tense but stable arrangement was what people call a happy life. To this end she had cultivated a shield of innocence and the thought patterns of a perpetual motion machine. With these defenses she tried not to notice how often she felt disappointed.

Painful as the resulting tension was for everyone involved, the arrangement was unshakable. Change was the last thing that any of the McGowans wanted. "We do not want to change" is usually the therapist's cue to say good-bye unless, like the McGowans themselves, the therapist is insecure, irritated, or in need of praise, or unless he is working for society to forcibly protect children, the suicidal, or the dangerously deranged. In the first of these instances, he is likely to waste time by trying to outsmart the patient (as I was doing), and in the second he may find himself providing a service more akin to social work than to therapy.

Almost two years after I met the McGowans, and some eighteen months after I'd stopped wasting everybody's time, Wanda's eyesight had deteriorated to the point where she was, in fact, legally blind. She could see enough to move around the house, but she could no longer drive, read, clean, or make her famous roll-ups. I was called back briefly to evaluate the situation.

Nothing appeared to have changed. Wanda showed me three large-print greeting cards from Lester with scratch-and-sniff pineapples, and I was supposed to say he was the most considerate son in the whole world. Lorrie was still into mirages—going downstairs for the mail and returning the next day—and dear, downtrodden Willis boasted a cane which suggested, as usual, that he could not provide quite as much help as was expected of him. In short, everyone continued to maintain the old illusion of mutual support while steering clear of anything as difficult as love.

The first hint that something was amiss was a "thank you" that Wanda let slip when Willis moved a bucket from her path.

Aha, I thought. What's this?

The hour passed, however, without further incident. Wanda still insisted that with her faith she could survive any of life's little disappointments. Now if Willis had gone blind, she confided in an audible whisper, he would have been devastated, because he was still a baby and couldn't take care of himself. Wanda did allow that Willis was learning to zap food in the microwave which Lester had sent against her express wishes, and that Willis also tried to clean but didn't know how. To be mean, Lorrie had hired a cleaning lady, but Wanda had met her at the top of the stairs and fired her on the spot. Willis wasn't going to get off that easy.

On my second visit, I surprised the McGowans in their small rose garden and heard them engaged in what sounded remarkably like the quiet and abbreviated exchange of intimates. They reverted to their former roles as soon as they saw me, but I noted that Wanda no longer rattled off her old complaints about Willis's messy flower beds. Of course, she couldn't see what he was doing anymore, and no one was foolish enough to tell her about the quarter acre of sodden newspapers that Willis had spread around the cabins for mulch. As for Willis himself, he accompanied us now as a matter of course to the upstairs parlor.

"Wanda relies on me a good deal," he told me later, when we were alone near the cars, in itself another departure. Wanda had not been able to abide the idea that anyone might want to converse alone with Willis because, as had become clear, she secretly believed that if anyone were nice to him for more than fifteen minutes he would offer to run away.

So talking with Willis alone was quite an event, and I began to suspect that failing vision might be accomplishing what neurotic discomfort and fitful therapy had never managed to achieve. When I learned that Willis had not yet moved out of the house and into one of the "summer cabins" where he had been in the habit of sleeping from May through September, I was certain that changes were under way.

Although both seemed determined not to notice what was happening, it appeared to me that blindness was forcing Wanda both to rely on Willis more and to let him go. The two actions seemed contradictory, but they were not. Willis was learning to cook, and he had taken over the books. Since Wanda could not look over his shoulder, he did things his way, and, although he still sighed a lot, he seemed somewhat proud of his efforts. He could even play Chinese checkers in the same room with Wanda now without being called stupid. He looked better, and I wondered if he was treating himself and Wanda to less of the old despondence. I felt better too. It was much easier to sit with Wanda and Willis now, perhaps because they had "mellowed," as the visiting nurse had told me earlier, or perhaps because I had stopped trying to change them.

"You look happier," I said to no one in particular as we sat for the last time in the parlor.

"Well, I'm pretty busy now," Willis answered slowly, "lot a hard work, but I don't miss the bad times when—"

"We've always been happy," interjected Wanda. "Willis is losing his memory."

"So you don't miss the good old days?"

"What? When we did everything together?" continued Wanda.

"No," I corrected, deciding to test the new freedom that I felt in the household, "when you used to take turns getting sick and when Willis stayed in the garage. You know, when you shouted back and forth."

Wanda was silent for about two seconds.

"Oh my dear," she laughed, the old giggle bursting again from deep in her throat. "You didn't *believe* us, did you? Oh, Willis," she gasped. "Did you hear? She thought . . ." And Wanda McGowan laughed with the most genuine hilarity I had ever heard in her voice. Between giggles and chokes, she finally regained control of her amusement. "You know, dear, it hasn't been easy, but Willis and I have always, *always* enjoyed a wonderful relationship."

"I'm glad to hear it," I said, marveling at the malleability of memory in Wanda's determined hands and getting no hint of confirmation or contradiction from Willis's nodding smile.

Wanda and Willis chuckled amiably together for a moment or

two over my foolishness, and I thought of all the useful lessons that this stubborn woman had taught me. Under her tutelage I had eventually stopped trying to outwit the no-win, no-change situations that characterized her household, and I had stopped being so unnerved by them. But the real lesson that I carried down two flights of stairs that afternoon was a genuine respect for the strength and seriousness of this awkward negotiation.

The Wandas of the world are not playing for small stakes. The no-win situations they construct with such a deep understanding of the human spirit represent their attempts to wrench allegiance from people whom they deeply suspect will never love them. They truly believe that if they let others decide for themselves how to treat them, these others will reject them. Thus they coerce husbands, wives, children, friends, and, of course, therapists—each with insecurities of his own—into treating them "right," and find they have won, at best, a Pyrrhic victory.

It is a common negotiation. Probably everyone grows up with enough doubts about himself to fear being rejected some of the time and thus to play into an occasional no-win situation. And a few people seem to have so little self-confidence that they all but wall themselves into a no-win life.

TURN OFF LIGHT I read at the bottom of the stairs as I let myself out.

KEEP DOOR SHUT.

The Man Who Had No Use for Words

[The second folly of Frederick the Great was] that he wanted to find out what kind of speech and what manner of speech children would have when they grew up, if they spoke to no one beforehand. So he bade foster mothers and nurses to suckle the children, to bathe and wash them, but in no way to . . . speak to them, for he wanted to learn whether they would speak the Hebrew language, which was the oldest, or Greek, or Latin, or Arabic, or perhaps the language of their parents. . . . The children all died for they could not live without . . . words.

the eighteenth-century
scholar SALALIMBENE

"I am not a talker," Mr. O'Reilly would say to me every couple of weeks, and indeed he was one of the most silent men I have ever met. In his fifty-nine years he seemed never to have found a use for words and, with the common sense that was one of his trademarks, he saw no reason to use them now. When others argued, he walked; when others prattled on among themselves or conversed with their own memories in dreams, he sat and smoked his pipe in the peaceful early hours of the morning—in the icy, starlit hours, in the pink-lined, bird-twittering hours between 3:00 and 6:00 A.M. It had been this way for a long time.

Mr. O'Reilly was born in Hillsdale into a family of six. Every Saturday evening, regardless of weather, his father climbed on his bicycle and rode to church. There he confessed, said his prayers, and walked back again, pushing his bicycle. On weekdays he said the rosary on his knees in front of a picture of the Blessed Mother, and on the first Friday of every month he said it twice.

The elder Mr. O'Reilly rarely spoke. Born in Ireland, he had emigrated first to Germany at the age of seven and had almost immediately gone to work in a quarry. Perhaps it was there that he lost the habit of speaking. As an adult—as a builder of fine walls—he never argued, never raised his hand against anyone, never drank, and no one in the family ever asked him why he rode to church and walked his bicycle home again every Saturday evening.

Mr. O'Reilly's mother was even tempered too. She worked hard, did not argue, but just once she became so silently enraged that she hit her youngest son on the hand.

The O'Reillys were not a happy family. They did not expect to be, and the idea, had it been put to them, would have seemed mildly offensive. Like good people everywhere, they had good times and hard times, and that was that.

I met Mr. O'Reilly during one of the hard times. His wife was ill with lupus, an unpredictable disease that had already begun to threaten her with slurring, staggering tumbles toward coma and death. She spent her days watching the soaps and saying the rosary. Mr. O'Reilly spent his watching Mrs. O'Reilly, except from 3:00 to 6:00 A.M., the hours of thoughtful dawn that he saved for himself and for contemplating his extensive collection of rocks.

As Mr. O'Reilly cared for his wife over the years, a problem of his own began to worsen. He was eventually diagnosed as having a particularly malevolent form of arthritis, and although he carried on in spite of it—once dragging his unconscious wife to the car on a toboggan when he could not carry her—he began to worry that he might lose the strength to care for her. The following spring, her crises mysteriously stopped, although they were still expected, and the couple settled down to wait—for her pains or his pains. As the grass turned green in the ditches along the roads around Hillsdale, Mr. O'Reilly began having the disagreeable sensation that he had swallowed a stone. It felt to him as if there were a hard lump of pure nervousness in the pit of his stomach. He finally sought treatment when he concluded that no medicine or exercise or prayer was going to dissolve that lump.

Thus, as a last resort, Mr. O'Reilly came to me, willing to try any treatment that would allow him to continue to care for his wife. He arrived, sat a safe distance away, and waited for me to melt the nervousness. What he did not do was speak.

For a few weeks I expected him to speak. I thought he would overcome whatever inhibitions he felt and get on with the business of telling me how he viewed his tense and lonely situation. But he did not. He answered yes and no respectfully, and sometimes, in answer to a question such as "How did you spend Christmas as a child?" he would blush like an ill-prepared student and admit that he simply did not know. Gradually I began to suspect that here was a man who did not have stories to tell about his life, not because his memory was poor but because he had not developed the habit of putting experience into words. It was as if he had not constructed any memories for himself out of the incidents he lived through, almost as if he had no use for words.

"Talking" with Mr. O'Reilly was an experience. Typically we sat in silence for several minutes, I wondering what the hour would bring, he rolling and rerolling his appointment card. He was an attractive man, although had I expressed this opinion I am sure he would have turned it aside with an embarrassed shake of his head. Nevertheless, he was a tall, sturdy man with powerful arms and shoulders. Before he got arthritis, I guessed that his had been an unusually straight and contained posture, and even now he tilted himself backward in his chair to compensate for the bowing of his head. He had a coarse but well-trained thatch of pure white hair which created what I always thought to be an invigorating contrast with his tanned skin. At the beginning of the hour his hands sometimes shook, and often he began our weekly exchange with a wordless apology, which he managed to convey with a shrug and a wry smile. We were off.

"Do you have any brothers and sisters, Mr. O'Reilly?" I remember asking in one of our early sessions.

"Yes."

And? I thought to myself. And?

And the silence filled the office like cotton batting. We were packed in silence, stuffed with silence. After a few more attempts to jump-start Mr. O'Reilly's memory, I resigned myself to a game of twenty questions.

"How many brothers and sisters?" "What are their ages?" "Their birth order?" "Do they have names?"

Slowly, a sort of outline of Mr. O'Reilly's life emerged, and I wasn't to know for months that it was mostly wrong. The picture that first came out was of an ordinary man. He claimed—if answering yes and no can be called claiming—to have grown up in an unremarkable family on the edge of town and to have passed uneventfully through childhood. He joined the air force, got married, worked hard in his father's trade, forgot to have children, took on the care of an ailing wife, and now, inexplicably, was weighted down with nervousness.

Although the majority of my early questions ran straight into his perplexed frown and embarrassed shrug, there were paths that were more actively barricaded. His parents were above criticism, for example. Also, he himself had no regrets ("Thy will be done"), his wife was approaching death peacefully, and Christmas was just like any other day of the year ("The hectic stuff I can do without"). On these topics there was no negotiation.

Yet, as the weeks passed, and winter locked the steep-roofed buildings of Mountain Valley into a glittering, snowy silence, another story crept into the first, giving to it a touch of color and a whisper of anguish. It seemed that Mr. O'Reilly had been a wild kid. As a five-year-old—a kindergartener—he began to smoke. By eight he was hitting cars with dirt balls, by ten he'd gotten himself kicked out of parochial school for pouring laundry soap in the heating system, and throughout the rest of his childhood he ran and scrapped and wrestled his way through every long country day. He alone of his brothers and sisters was a continual troublemaker.

At some unremembered age, he himself began to wonder why he was so relentlessly rebellious. At first he tried to atone for his contrariness by building small shrines in the woods behind his house. The art of arranging rocks came naturally to him, it seemed, and, although he could not explain it precisely, the heft and roughness of fieldstone in his hands had always calmed him down. As he put it, "Rocks are rocks."

Nevertheless, the solitary moving around of rocks did not prove a sufficient balm for his remorse, and, as the intense and muscular Mr. O'Reilly skidded into adolescence, he increasingly tried to behave like the other members of his family. Impressed no doubt by the overwhelming earnestness of a father who prayed before the Virgin, and of siblings who attended Mass every day in parochial school, he too developed the habit of prayer.

"Sometimes I prayed for a happy death," he said matter-of-factly, and for me—not him—the myth of an ordinary childhood fell apart. Mostly, he continued, he prayed for self-control and failed. At fifteen he left home and apprenticed himself to a stonemason in a monastery. However, even this kind and quiet atmosphere could not give the young Mr. O'Reilly the self-control he desired. It did not turn him into a replica of his father. He dimly remembered feeling shut up, as if in a large, silent thermos bottle.

"Maybe I was getting homesick."

After nearly two years of what in retrospect seems a misguided exercise in denial for a strapping teenage boy, Mr. Reilly walked into the refectory and called home.

"Pick me up."

"What time?"

"Four P.M."

"And surely your father asked you why," I said, pleading with the long-dead elder O'Reilly. "Surely he did not simply meet you at the monastery and not ask you anything."

"Yes."

"And? And then?"

"And then we drove home."

Several minutes of silence passed in the small office, and Mr. O'Reilly added, "After a week I became so tired I couldn't get out of bed—just couldn't. My mother called the doctor. I was sleeping . . . , and he took me away."

Mr. O'Reilly joined the air force shortly after leaving the monastery, and no one thought the transition ironic.

During the next eight years Mr. O'Reilly hit upon two plans for driving the devil from his soul. Stationed on an air force base in Alaska, he worked furiously and, like his father, developed the reputation of doing twice as much as anyone else. In his free time he took up weight lifting and wrestling. At first he confined these silent endeavors to the gym, but as the unacknowledged strain of loneliness grew, he began fighting with other restless men first on the flight line and then in downtown dives. He could not remember why he fought, or who, and when I suggested that he might have found a passionate release in grappling his way through a crowd of drunks just as earlier he had erupted through the streets and fields of Hillsdale, he shrugged. In any event, he admitted earning the reputation of being a tough, quick fighter with a short fuse. The strength he acquired in his upper body, he added, stood him in good stead when he went into business for himself building walls.

In addition to taming himself with physical exertion, Mr. O'Reilly married a woman who already knew how to be a mother. He expected that with the experience she'd gained by raising her sister's four children for as many years, she would know how to calm him down. At twenty-one he was ready to be somebody's "old man."

When Mr. O'Reilly decided to marry, he was in the Matanuska Valley. He spent nearly eight years there, assigned to a maintenance crew, and one afternoon he struck up a conversation with an Indian girl who sold gold-nugget jewelry at the base exchange. Her name in Aleutian meant "forget-me-not," and he liked the way she smiled.

Mr. O'Reilly remembered the eighteen months of his courtship much the way he remembered the rest of his life—in fragments. By this time our sessions had progressed somewhat beyond the twenty questions format, and I felt that he trusted me enough at least to humor my baffling need to question. Nevertheless, only incidents, rather than stories, emerged. A meeting, a decision, another tour of duty amid endless days and nights—his memories were like a bag of beads that had come unstrung or, I suspected, that had never been laced on the strings of his soul. Thus we hopped through his years in Alaska with a disconcerting lack of continuity, until we landed for just a moment at the edge of a town several miles from the base.

Here we found Mr. and Mrs. O'Reilly, now apparently married, living in a house overlooking the bay and walking their dog in the morning. For an instant, Mr. O'Reilly seemed to feel his own past, and, although he used only two or three sentences to describe the scene, it sang to me. His "black-sand beach in the early morning" and "steep, green hills" blossomed instantly in my mind. I seemed suspended high above a curving, jet black beach, and far below me walked the young O'Reillys and their rambunctious dog. I saw them turn away from the water and start along a narrow trail flanked by shrubbery still wet from the morning rain and fragrant with flowers. I wondered if they spoke. And it seemed to me in that moment—and would again in later weeks—that Mr. O'Reilly was wise to be wary of remembering. Earlier, a few of his unstrung beads had revealed the sadness of his silent childhood, and now a glimpse of something akin to joy had shaken loose and might unbalance his account of his middle years.

About this time Mr. O'Reilly decided to leave therapy. The stone in his stomach was getting smaller, and he felt he had gotten what he came for. Although he had indeed learned to reduce tension by talking, I pointed out that we had only just begun to identify the source of the stress. Yes, he said, threading what appeared to be new knowledge back into his past, he'd "always known" that getting things off his chest made him feel better, but enough was enough.

We had the only real fight of our acquaintanceship then, a jumbled concoction composed of half a dozen layers. Would he leave or stay? Lead or follow? Open or close? Dig or cover? But the issue with the power to enrage had deeper roots. As I argued for what I hoped he heard as flexibility, curiosity, expansion, affection, and living, for God's sake, *just living,* I felt increasingly like the wild kid. Yet as I darted around his arguments, encircling his thoughts with my own, I felt the massive fairness and piety of his arguments weigh me down. He was as immovable as God, as imperturbable as a monastery or a stone wall—perhaps as imperturbable as his silent parents. I was stopped cold by all this heavy, quiet righteousness, and I was fuming. It would have been an indulgence of the most delicious kind to throw a screaming, raging fit. I could taste it. Instead, we looked at each other across the short landscape of rugs and chairs that lay between us and repeated the parting ritual. "See you next week, Mr. O'Reilly." "Yup."

On the way home I wondered if he would indeed leave in the next several weeks and, if so, how he would readjust to the tension. "I can handle it," he had told me. "When it gets too bad, I drive down to Silver Pond and add to the wall."

"Add to the wall?" I repeated.

Mr. O'Reilly blushed. "I've always liked building walls when things get bad," he explained. "It's quiet."

Perhaps because of the arthritis which slowed his gait and gave to his once strong hands something of a paddlelike quality, I could not quite picture Mr. O'Reilly standing in the woods near Silver Pond wrestling old rocks from the ground and fitting them into a wall that wandered aimlessly toward the water. But what I could imagine now were slabs of rock that stood for wordless pain.

Mr. O'Reilly arrived the following week and said simply, "I'll dig." What he apparently meant was that he would continue therapy for eight weeks and do his best in that time not to let me rock his boat. At first I tried to go back over events we'd already touched on, looking, I believed, for important but previously forgotten facts. I soon discovered, however, that the contract had changed, and we were doing more restoring than remodeling. His goal seemed to be to put his life back into the orderly pattern he had first presented, and since even the most common historic facts of his life had a negotiable existence, they were recast again to this end. A great general contracting scheme that had metamorphosed in the telling into a family feud between him and two brothers reverted to its original status as an inspired enterprise. The best vacation he and his wife had ever taken—a curious boozy interlude in Miami—became again a present to his wife which no longer expressed in its uncharacteristic flamboyance the enormity of his remorse.

Steady became his favorite word in these weeks, and he would list the improvements he had made in his life since his wife fell ill. He had given up drinking. There was no more fighting—neither on the job nor in bars at night—no swearing, and soon, he hoped, there would be no more smoking, although this sacrifice still eluded him during his early-morning vigils. Indeed, his steadiness (and inaccessibility) visibly increased, and for five weeks he moved relentlessly back toward the masklike silence he had cultivated all his life.

As so often happens, however, Mr. O'Reilly was disarmed by the sight of land. Believing himself safely within reach of the end of therapy, he relaxed his vigilance and gave away those insignificant secrets that frequently explain the pattern of a life. We had talked before about his wife, Forget-me-not O'Reilly, and I had been given a collection of facts about her as poorly connected as the rest of Mr. O'Reilly's memories. Kiki, as she was called, had weighed 106 pounds when they were married—there was not much left now; she had always been outgoing; she never learned to drive her husband's standard-shift truck; she was happy; she always drank from her own glass, and once, when he had used it by mistake, she became so enraged that she smashed it on the floor.

She had no regrets; and on several vacations she had played the pinball machines for hours with a desperate passion that attracted crowds. Once, in Atlantic City, she set a record for winning seven and a half hour's worth of free games on her favorite Joe Bazooka machine.

But now, in the last weeks, Mr. O'Reilly admitted matter-of-factly that Kiki was sometimes irritable. She would never say what was wrong, but her resentful silence returned the stone to his stomach. As an example he described how he had been getting up at 3:00 A.M. these cool spring mornings to sit and smoke his pipe on the screen porch. Around him lay cartons of rocks, some from Ireland and Germany, some from Alaska, some rough and pitted, some smooth and polished, and each a perfect model of inarticulate endurance.

Mr. O'Reilly knew that Kiki did not like him to get up before dawn and guessed (since she would never say more than "Why so early?") that she felt less able to sleep once he had left their bed.

"Does she feel lonely?" I asked. "Abandoned?"

"No. I haven't gone anywhere. Besides, she would never say that."

"And if she did? If she said, 'Please come back to bed and stay with me. Please love me.'"

Mr. O'Reilly sat in silence. He began to sweat. In three excruciating minutes sweat was running down his face so fast that it collected in pools above his collarbones. I could watch it spill into his shirt when he moved.

Quietly, then, he described how he had been unable to go with his wife to get the results of tests that confirmed her diagnosis. He had seen the desperation in her eyes, and no words were needed to tell him how afraid she was, how in need of comfort, how desperate for love. But he had sent her off with a neighbor. He had stayed home and cried for only the third time in his entire life. He never told his wife this, and afterward he felt a need to raise the quarry-stone wall around their property by about two feet and redouble his guard. "I have always had to protect myself," he mused. "I protect us all."

So there it was. The man who protected himself with rocks and silence, the man who had no use for words, and no words for feelings of anger or of passion, did not speak for fear he would hear the crying of his own heart and that of his wife's. To speak with feeling would be to ache again for love, yearn for children, and burn with indignation. Above all, it would be to weep for his wife's loneliness and his own, to grieve openly—as he had grieved silently all his life—for his own inability to love his wife, or himself, as each had wished to be loved. I wondered then, as I watched the color recede from his flushed face and the sweating abate, if his whole family had not suffered the same tangential connection to their own hearts. Had all the O'Reillys been unwilling to speak for the same fear of learning too much? And had the pious elder O'Reilly ridden his bicycle to church on Saturdays to confess to an imperfect numbness, which, like his son, he had somehow confused with goodness? Both of these stoneworkers prayed for the day when all their desires would cease and they could wall themselves into an honorable submission. Neither seemed to have understood that the wildness in their natures—the problem—was also the fuel that built their shrines.

"Since she's been sick I've been steady," continued Mr. O'Reilly, "but it's like being beaten up. Sometimes I hurt so much I can't speak."

"And sometimes you hurt so much you can't hear either," I added, and I felt the sadness that comes from not being able to give the words that could reanimate the part of his life that he had worked so hard to immobilize.

We sat in silence. Outside the office window, the sunlight filtered through the succulent spring greens of larch and maple, and I wondered what became of those foster mothers in Frederick's time who were not allowed to sing to their babies.

Memories Left in the Heart

There is nothing higher and stronger and more wholesome and good for life in the future than some good memory, especially a memory of childhood, of home. . . . If one carries many such memories into life, one is safe to the end of one's days, and if one has only one good memory left in one's heart, even that may be the means of saving us.

FYODOR DOSTOEVSKY,
The Brothers Karamazov

Four miles north of Hillsdale, a glacial erratic of considerable size balances on smaller rocks like a schooner poised on the crest of a wave, and it is in this region of stony, unpromising farms that Ivan Sibeski goes in search of a usable past. Whereas others, at a time of loss, might sift through their own memories and thus contrive to explain to themselves the inexplicable turns of their lives, Mr. Sibeski rolls through the frozen swells of the countryside looking for signs of plant and animal life. It is a quiet wager he is making, both painful and beautiful to watch.

Leaving his cabin before dawn, he wheels himself along the

outskirts of town and turns onto a quiet back road near an old barn. The hunt is on. Gliding through snowy woods poised on the edge of spring, Mr. Sibeski goes back in time a year or more with every rhythmic push of his powerful arms. Only yards from the main road he has entered a more congenial time.

He is an astute observer of these largely abandoned farms. As if his life depended on taking note of every track and call and scent, or as if he believed he were seeing these woods for the last time, he drinks in his surroundings with a thirst that is difficult to comprehend. From the tracks of mink and rabbit near a frozen stream he calculates each animal's weight and from this the probable source and amount of food available to each. From the smell of woodsmoke drifting up from the valley he knows who is burning hardwood and who has turned to pine. He notes that the buds on the wild blueberry are still red, those of the beech a pointed yellow-green. He sees a hawk. He sees the golden pollen of catkins on the white snow. He memorizes everything.

Only when the four o'clock sun slides down the clustered trunks of maples does Mr. Sibeski leave the farmlands. He turns his back on the surveyors' stakes that he has seen march in from the far fields up to and through the old farms themselves. He heads for the edge of town. Taking a last look, he sees peacefulness all around him but cannot feel it. What he can feel, he tells me, is overwhelming loss.

Nineteen years after Ivan Sibeski returned from an abbreviated tour in the tidal waters of Vietnam, he nearly succeeded in drinking himself to death. Bombarded by an incalculable number of beers, the lining of his stomach wore out. He lost thirty pounds in one month and bled every time he threw up. When he wheeled himself into his doctor's office, he was told to go to the hospital if he wanted to live more than two weeks. He thought about it for ten days, then checked himself in. Something in the frozen look of terror on his rocky face made his doctor refuse to release him until he signed up for therapy at one of the clinics in Mountain Valley Hospital.

Thirty-nine years old to the day, Ivan Sibeski rolled into my office. Dressed in clean jeans and a gray sweatshirt, torn at the neck to allow his muscular neck and shoulders to move freely, he spun his wheelchair expertly through the door and parked himself as far away from my desk as he could tactfully manage. He was—or had been—an exceptionally tall man, and now he sat like a boulder at one end of my office. Beneath straight blond hair tied neatly in a ponytail, his features stepped down his face like ledges. His brow was prominent, his hooked nose large yet perfectly proportioned, his mouth wide and thin. As long as I knew him I was entranced by his looks.

Mr. Sibeski certainly did not believe that he needed a therapist. Nevertheless, he agreed to see me one or more times a week for several months until his system had adjusted to the absence of alcohol. No doubt he would feel a little better every day, he believed, and if there were a problem, like flashbacks and nightmares, for instance, well, no big deal.

During the first weeks of our acquaintance, Mr. Sibeski gave me a severely censored account of his life. He had grown up outside Hillsdale, the younger of two boys. His father had briefly taught Russian literature at a distant community college before returning to a more ordinary and convenient occupation. His mother he remembered less clearly. "I guess because she stayed indoors most of the time, and I was out." He had wanted to be a soldier of fortune, he told me, ever since his father "brought *War and Peace* home with him," and, true to his dream, he had enlisted in the army at the age of eighteen and volunteered for the Mobile Riverine Force. After training, he spent seven months in Vietnam as a "river rat wading in oatmeal." At the end, he had been hit in the back by an ammunition locker and sent home. The accident did not seem serious at the time but had resulted in progressive damage that years later made walking or standing for more than a few minutes impossible. Mr. Sibeski then turned his old love of running into long-distance wheeling and eventually became so proficient in his wheelchair that people told him they forgot he was handicapped.

Now, he continued, he was dismayed to be feeling "on the edge" again, as he had in Vietnam. Awake, his mind raced and he felt jumpy and vigilant. Asleep, he had nightmares. The smell of diesel exhaust was a particularly potent reminder, and he could not pass a fuel oil truck without "going back." To counteract this edginess, he was spending more and more time by himself and taking longer trips around Hillsdale in his light wheelchair. He had a few friends, sort of, thought of his brother, sometimes, and would prefer not to answer so many questions. It was no big deal, he assured me, but they made him "uncomfortable as hell."

Approximately one month into therapy and sobriety, Mr. Sibeski arrived at my office in an extremely agitated condition. Sweat glistened above his sweatshirt, and his hands, usually so sure, slipped once or twice as he guided his chair into the room. Because there had been a thaw, he explained, he had gone for a ride in the farmlands and had stopped near a stand of oaks to watch thin squirrels forage for acorns. For a long time he watched them dart down the oaks, dig through the soft snow, then scamper back up the trees or across the road. As he was about to leave, a car came up over the hill. Almost predictably, a squirrel darted into the road, froze, reversed its course, and was hit. Thrown to the side of the road, the animal churned frantically through the snow like a fizzling rocket, then lay dead. It was over in three seconds, Mr. Sibeski told me, but in that time he had apparently launched himself from his wheelchair into a ditch and grabbed a rock "the size of a grenade."

Mr. Sibeski was now shaking, and tears glistened in his eyes.

"I was shaking so hard I couldn't get back in my chair," he finally said and added softly, "I wanted to kill every person in that car."

Mr. Sibeski then described for me his first really horrible experience in Vietnam. His unit had proceeded through a marshland to a tidal flat that now lay some two feet under gently swirling water. A half-submerged box of K rations was spotted fifty yards away, and draped over the box was what looked like the body of an American soldier.

"Sibeski, bring in that fucking box," ordered the captain, who, in Sibeski's opinion, was a dumb and therefore dangerous leader.

"Sir," answered Sibeski. He then squatted down and looked hard across the water.

"Sibeski!" bellowed the captain.

"Sir, I think it's a trap. The—"

"I do the fucking thinking, Sibeski."

Before Sibeski could reply, the captain had ordered a tall, skinny kid into the water. The new recruit slogged his way through the warm, brown water until, some four feet away from his target, he inadvertently set off the mine. With a roar, pieces of the skinny kid and of the dummy the VC had draped across the box went up into the air together in a geyser of blood.

Sibeski, now lying flat in the marsh grass like the rest of his company, was momentarily startled by the sound of rain. Looking up, he saw flesh and splinters and water pattering down on his silent comrades.

"Coward!" the captain suddenly shrieked, leaping to his feet. "You goddamned fucking, know-it-all coward!"

In one of the few very clear memories that Mr. Sibeski retained of his years in Vietnam—or so he thought—he remembered feeling his own blood explode into his head like the geyser sent by the mine. The captain's face, his comrade's face, the faces in a tight ring looking on around him spun wildly in a red blur. Impulsively, he grabbed with one hand for the pistol on his belt, and with the other he grabbed the captain. He intended, he told me, to shoot the captain and then himself. As with the squirrel episode, however, he began to shake so violently that he was unable to get the pistol out of its holster.

He needed to stop shaking, he said.

I looked across the room at Ivan Sibeski, who had so completely regained control of his emotions that he again reminded me of a geological formation.

"Why now?" I think I asked, intrigued by his desire to eliminate the reaction that had once saved his life.

"Because I'm losing ground," he replied.

Over the next several weeks it became increasingly clear that the lid was in danger of blowing off the volcano. Memories and emotions that Mr. Sibeski, like so many others, had first deflected with the immediate necessity of staying alive, then drowned with alcohol, were no longer remaining out of mind. His strategy, it seemed, was to face these returning emotions and throw them forcibly from his mind. Eventually he would argue himself into a life that was free from the past or die honorably in the attempt. His only allies were the fields and farms of Hillsdale, and from these he hoped to wring some solitary comfort before memories of Vietnam drove him over the edge. Such was his gamble.

It was not mine. I had learned from others and had discovered for myself that fear is not often faced down by solitary combat. Instead, I was betting on a cycle of reconnecting and remembering, the two activities Mr. Sibeski disliked the most. From my perspective, the treatment of choice was for Mr. Sibeski to talk with other Vietnam veterans and, in discovering that his feelings of horror and remorse were not unique to him, to gain a sense of camaraderie. At the same time I was hoping that he would feel supported enough to go back in his mind to his childhood and find among what I dimly suspected were painful memories the remnants of love, those memories Dostoevsky spoke of "that may be the means of saving us."

With these thoughts in mind, I found myself in a curious three-way race. The most dramatic contestant was terror, and daily this force seemed to engage more and more of Mr. Sibeski's mind. The terror came as nightmares—"old familiar ones," new ones—as nameless dread, as particular fears, and, at odd moments, as something that began to feel like paranoia. Pitted against the terror were Mr. Sibeski's stoic attempts to shut out the past and my insistence on letting it back in. Each of us worked hard—and at cross-purposes—to marshal our forces against the nightmares.

"How have you been?" I would typically ask at the beginning of each session.

"All right. . . . Not bad," he would answer, and we would beat around the bush in a companionable way until he decided what parts of his pain he would and would not reveal.

"I had a new nightmare last night."

"Umm?"

Mr. Sibeski shuddered. "I was crouched in a shower stall—on the base, I guess, and there was a field radio in there with me with all its wires hanging out. The water kept pouring over me—into my eyes and ears—and I was trying to jam the wires back in to tell them I was coming. I knew I had to *be* someplace, but I was trapped. Outside, I could see the Vietcong swarming up telephone poles and cutting the wires. They were swinging into the locker room, using the phone wires like vines. They were crawling under the doors too."

"And then?"

He shuddered again. "I always wake up just before the damage is done."

Soon I, too, could distinguish between the "old familiar nightmares" and the new ones. Jammed guns, empty guns. Hiding places that were flooded by the incoming tide, comrades who stood up too soon. Marshland that turned into abandoned farms, high school football fields that turned into rice paddies. And always Mr. Sibeski was one millimeter or one split second away from a gruesome and dishonorable death, and always he woke drenched with sweat, determined to drive these thoughts back to the dungeons of his mind. To outflank his dreams, he postponed going to sleep until two, then three in the morning. He slept less. He kept a light on. But the nightmares tore through his mind no matter how hard he concentrated on other things.

Of course, everyone's past and present tumble together in dreams, but in Mr. Sibeski's case it seemed as if the horror and rage—the Vietnam part of the dreams—had a way of ensnaring the countryside of Hillsdale in a particularly malevolent manner. Symbols of Vietnam and of the present didn't simply coexist; the former actively took root in his present life and grew at its expense. The nightmares even drew Mr. Sibeski's wheelchair and damaged legs back into Vietnam. The dreams consumed everything they touched. They ate his mind.

Pitted against this process were some pitiful advances in the opposite direction. These consisted only in the reclaiming of lost memories, for initially Mr. Sibeski would have nothing to do with the other half of my prescription, namely, befriending other veterans. So we worked with memories, and I learned, for example, that the elder Mr. Sibeski was a hardworking man—one might say driven—who was hugely admired by his sons for all the things he knew and all the stories he could tell from books. In spite of this precious education, however, the elder Sibeski insisted on a simple life and seemed happiest when he was busy. He left for work before the rest of the family got up in the morning and returned home late in the afternoon and showered again. Most evenings he walked downtown to the library or a bar and grill. Ivan remembered lying in bed before dawn listening to the shower running, and later, after school, hearing the water splashing again against the metal stall. "Sometimes I pretended he had been in the shower all day," he mused. "I still think of my father when I hear a heavy rain."

Mr. Sibeski's mother remained a more shadowy figure, for reasons that were not yet clear to me, but her son could recall a certain sparkle in her eye or perhaps a vitality in her voice when she was speaking Polish with her mother and father at Easter. She got up to cook then, too. It was her favorite holiday. As the years passed, however, she ate less and drank more. Her face began to thin. Her husband adored her.

When Ivan was twelve and finishing sixth grade in a school he claimed to have forgotten entirely, he returned home at dusk having taken the long way home through miles of woods and farmlands. His mother was up, which was unusual, and as he climbed the porch steps his brother punched his fist through the storm door and ran off down the street, leaving drops of blood on the porch.

There was a long silence in the office.

"After my father's wake, I never went back," said Mr. Sibeski.

"His wake?" I repeated.

"He died of a heart attack at home, right after work, and we had to stand in a funeral parlor for two days . . . I never went back to the cemetery or the drugstore."

Apparently the memories associated with both of these places were too painful for Mr. Sibeski to bear, and he had done his best to avoid unmanageable sadness by ignoring them both. Judging from the further restrictions he had placed on his life and the quantity of childhood memories he had forgotten, many other places and situations triggered feelings of sadness as well. And indeed they did. That same year Ivan's dog, Mr. Wizard, was hit by a car in front of the house, and his mother and older brother began arguing in the kitchen. In an embarrassingly painful attempt to fill her husband's role, Mrs. Sibeski had briefly emerged from her room and tried to keep a "family diary." As her sons made themselves sandwiches for dinner, she sat in the middle of the kitchen and carefully transcribed what she had long hoped they would want to say. It drove Ivan's brother wild.

By the end of the following year, the family was splitting up. Ivan's brother ran away, and Ivan was sent to stay for days and then weeks at a time with a neighbor. Mrs. Sibeski apparently returned to her own thoughts and became increasingly depressed.

Ivan, too, tried to cope with loss and confusion by tuning out. He attended school less and less and finally dropped out. Eventually he was enticed into pursuing the rough equivalent of a work-study program, which gave him just enough change to buy *Field & Stream* magazines and just enough credits to get a high school diploma. Both at work and at school he kept strictly to himself, however, and only felt comfortable alone in the woods.

Perhaps it was his love of tracking and the old habit of reading magazines in the library that combined to interest him in Vietnam. He was fascinated by the country's history, economy, and geography. Fascinated even more by the endless waterways and by the cat-and-mouse games that a sharp-witted hunter might play there in the mangrove swamps. On his eighteenth birthday he joined the army, determined to go to Vietnam. At last there was something to live for.

Intrigued by this hint of former vitality, I nudged Mr. Sibeski toward an encounter with his feelings by asking him to record the thoughts that tramped through his mind at midnight. I had used this procedure before to good effect. He produced a curious chronicle. Roughly half the pieces he wrote were on Vietnam, and to my astonishment these were full of brilliant blue skies, lush riverbanks, and patrol boats bedecked with young, sweating soldiers. Strength radiated from these snapshots, and they were clean. Interleafed with them, however, were bleak accounts of life in Hillsdale. A late-winter storm rattled dark windows. Trees were trapped in ice. Streets, nights, fields—all were empty.

These memories, far from producing the more balanced account of his life that I was hoping for, were doing the opposite. For one thing, all his experience was being polarized into an ideal-but-gone-forever category or a horrible-and-ever-present one. For another, the emotions I expected him to associate with his past were being reversed. Vietnam emerged as a country of exquisite warmth where eighteen- and nineteen-year-old heroes lived by their wits, but Hillsdale was barren and beyond redemption. Clearly we were not tapping that "good memory" that might breathe some hope into Mr. Sibeski's present life, nor were we discussing the powerful details of specific events that could give him a truer picture of his time in Vietnam. In short, we were not making much progress, and the terror was gaining.

Mr. Sibeski began having what he called "the tube-worm nightmare," only he had it when he was wide awake. First he felt as if he were being drawn into a trance. Dread and dizziness mounted. He grew short of breath. As he struggled to breathe, his vision began to contract, and by the time he broke into a drenching sweat, he was peering down a tube that reminded him of those that the tube worm builds on the bottoms of boats. Still his field of vision contracted until it was the size of a dime, and something told Mr. Sibeski that if the tube closed completely he would die. At first, he fought with all his strength to "wake up" before the tube closed, but now, he told me, he had decided to just let it happen. (Inadvertently, he had hit upon an excellent antidote for his panic attacks, and once he stopped fighting them, they abated.)

Nonetheless, I was beginning to be alarmed by a number of things. For one thing, he was no longer seeing anyone, not even his sometime friend Roger. For another, he told me that he was dreading the day when he would have to get his prescription for sleeping pills refilled. He was sure the pharmacist thought he was an alcoholic looking for drugs to substitute for his lost beer. Moreover, they probably believed he had disgraced his country. Mr. Sibeski also told me that he could no longer bear to look at himself in the mirror, partly because he didn't recognize the face he saw there and partly because he was afraid that "the shell" was "inhabited." He stopped shaving. I doubled our usual number of sessions.

In April, spring shambled into Hillsdale, and Mr. Sibeski began to remember a great deal more about both Vietnam and his childhood. Perhaps it was our conversations, perhaps those long trips he was taking in his wheelchair, voraciously noting everything he saw, but in any case he now formed the habit of playing scenes of the local countryside over and over in his head during the evening. His intention was to ward off memories of Vietnam, but he also seemed to be inviting memories back from his childhood, and these would insinuate themselves into his thoughts of open cornfields. Now he remembered his mother and father arguing. His father was always tired from working. His mother wanted to go out to a park, to a restaurant, for a drive, to a movie. Perhaps she was bored and lonely, Mr. Sibeski surmised. Perhaps disappointed. In any event, he could now recall that she was definitely spending more time in her room. The arguments got worse. The trips to the park stopped. He and his brother ate alone in the kitchen. He remembered that his brother had been crying as he ran down the steps. His mother had been crying too. Everyone cried except him.

Mr. Sibeski remembered more about his tour of duty too, although this was not his intention. The memories were not so nice now, but we both noticed that they carried with them a certain gritty and almost comforting specificness that had been lacking in his earlier idealized memories, which, like his nightmares, seemed unsettlingly vague. (Again inadvertently, he had hit upon another method of reducing anxiety—namely, picturing a threat in detail rather than leaving it a nebulous and unmanageable terror.) He now remembered seeing flamethrowers scorch the underbrush along the waterways, and seeing a dog that looked like Mr. Wizard roasted by those twin streams of fire. He remembered mud, too, miles and miles of stinking mud. And, even without closing his eyes, he saw again the Vietcong trooper standing in the reeds at the edge of a canal firing at Sibeski's patrol. Saw the look on the thin, strange face when, with his clip empty, the VC spotted Sibeski in the mud behind a Stoner carbine and knew his life was over. Sibeski remembered how the body tumbled into the canal and how, when its slow downstream progress was stopped by a tangle of roots, the blood around it kept on flowing.

He remembered too coming home and ducking into the men's room in the airport to change out of his treasured uniform so that no one would spit on him. Remembered coming into the kitchen at Hillsdale and being asked by a neighbor what it was like to kill a man. He would have had to draw his loaded .45 and hold it to his head to give him even the first shivering scream of real under-standing.

This kind of remembering finally began to get us somewhere. In fact, it ushered in a period of all-but-unmanageable progress, for attached to each new memory was a great deal of emotion, mainly rage. For reasons that were not clear to me, Mr. Sibeski continued to feel in his dreams that he had let his country down, but upon awaking he was now a soldier betrayed by the massive insensitivity of his own country. He was an incandescently furious victim. Curiously, however, he was loath to mention personal disappoint-ments. He preferred to be furious in behalf of others who had suffered, rather than express the anger or the hurt for himself and rail against the bad things that had happened to him. I surmised that, like other veterans I had worked with, he still felt guilty enough about something that had happened in Vietnam to believe that he did not have the right to complain. In addition, it seemed that his memories were returning in stages. First came the incidents themselves, but in a somewhat disembodied way. Then came specific memories, which triggered tremendous emotion, but in behalf of other people. And third—at least I hoped this was the next step—came memories straight from his own heart.

For a month or more, however, Mr. Sibeski seemed stuck in a rage he could neither accept nor ignore. He reported getting what he called "that mission feeling," as if he were getting ready to go on patrol. He knew there was something "out there" he had to do. He was reluctant to describe these thoughts, which he erroneously believed were unique to him, for fear I would think him crazy and try to hospitalize him. Nonetheless, he gradually let me know that a plot was afoot to test his courage once and for all. He had realized that there was some action he must undertake for others. He felt as if some alien force were pushing him deeper and deeper.

"Into enemy territory?" I ventured.

"Yes," he replied, surprised by my answer. "I dreamt about that last night. I could see the Vietcong coming down from the northwest along the Saigon River. I was shadowing them, in a canoe or something, but moving in the opposite direction. I couldn't stop myself."

"And could it be that the strong feelings you have about your mother and father, about the captain who tried to make you cross the water, about your lost comrades—that all these feelings also represent a kind of enemy territory into which you are walking?"

"No," he replied politely. "Something has been planted in me, awakened. The enemy is out there.

"You know," he added after a pause, "I have lost my ability to control what I see and hear. I see *into* people now. I hear their motives. . . . I see and hear too much."

With this I silently agreed and wondered how much longer this sleepless, driven man could hold out against some form of mental and physical collapse.

Mr. Sibeski looked like death itself when he weakly pushed himself into my office several days later. He was carrying an old jacket in his lap, and for an instant it looked to me like the remains of his own body. We did not beat around the bush. "The mission feeling" had peaked two days before, Mr. Sibeski told me. After overhearing a conversation in town about a landowner who was selling out to a Vietnamese entrepreneur, he had suddenly realized that the dozens of odd little clues and feelings he had noticed in the past months made sense. They all pointed to an obvious plot. He suddenly understood that the wealthy "gook" was buying up cabins on the outskirts of town, where veterans like Sibeski himself could afford to live. The developer was planning to plow the area under and build weekend chalets for yuppie trash. Then he'd start on the farms. The stakes were already in the ground.

Sibeski knew he had been singled out to stop the project. Methodically he had begun to make his plans. Carrying the local paper that described the project with him, he wheeled past the land that was for sale. Accustomed to picking out wildlife, he had found it difficult at first to find what he was looking for, but eventually he counted a dozen antennae-topped bungalows nestled among thickets of abandoned refrigerators, washers, and transmissions.

"I marked every location on a map." (I had known he was near the edge the week before. Should I have tried to hospitalize him then?) Next he staked out the real estate office that was handling the sale, and identified the buyer's car. (Christ, why hadn't I seen this coming?) On the second day, he cleaned and loaded his gun.

"Oh, Jesus!"

Mr. Sibeski raised his blond head and gave me a quizzical look.

"Before I went out," he continued, "I had this funny feeling that I wanted to touch something that belonged to my father."

Thus before stalking the "gook," Mr. Sibeski dragged out an old carton of his father's books. From it he took Vladimir Nabokov's memoirs and saw in its pages, both literally and figuratively, a snapshot of himself. Marking a passage in which Nabokov's mother teaches her son how to store memories of what he would shortly lose, was a photograph of skinny, ten-year-old Ivan at 4-H camp. It reminded him of the letters he had received then from his father—the only letters he had ever received in his life.

As Mr. Sibeski looked at himself in the snapshot and read the passage, he found himself floating back into his own past on Nabokov's passionate memories of a lost homeland. A distracted feeling of affection for his family began to return. He imagined the sound of rain.

"That passage made me think," he continued. "It isn't the gooks who are taking away our old way of life. They don't know what's happening. It's a kind of crumbling that's going on . . . inside and outside."

Too weak to reply myself but silently thanking the memory of a loving if largely absent father even more than Nabokov, I listened while Mr. Sibeski described the night that followed his decision not to kill the "gook." Tormented by the prospect of nightmares, he had taken to sitting up most nights in his wheelchair. He would take a sleeping pill about two in the morning, then let himself fall out of his chair onto the floor when sleep finally overtook him. There he would sleep for two or three hours, until the nightmares came. This particular night, however, sleep did not come at all. A tightness started in his shoulders and spread to his neck and head. By midnight, it felt as if his head were locked in a vise. Thoughts of Vietnam clattered and banged through his mind, and beneath the noise Mr. Sibeski could hear—or rather sense—the low drone of approaching fear.

Mr. Sibeski resisted with all his might. He countered with reasonableness every charge of cowardice that memory threw at him. He fought against despair by insisting he was strong. He forced himself to think of Hillsdale. And he told himself the pill would put him to sleep any minute now, before he went crazy, please, before his head imploded. Still a flood of thoughts washed him back to Vietnam to hear again the sound of mortars—the whine, the resonant thump—to see along the riverbanks rolling blankets of fire, to feel again the burdensome heat. For the hundredth time he saw the newly married nineteen-year-old stand up too soon—the kid he had told never to undress while on duty, the kid who stood like an illuminated target in his white skivvies. And for the thousandth time he heard men screaming for their mothers—the last call, the deepest memory. And how he hated that ripping memory.

Mr. Sibeski did not sleep that night, but even awake his battered consciousness could not hold off the memory that fueled the "main nightmare." Once again he lay half-buried in mud between the prop roots of a mangrove tree—a dangerous place, he had told me earlier, full of snakes and leeches. It was night and the heavy air was full of insects that drifted in off the sluggish canal in front of him and gathered in clouds around his head. Because he knew exactly where to look, he could see the shadowy outline of his comrade squatting on the opposite side of the canal. Their unit was camped downstream. Their job was to watch for Vietcong, who knew and used these waterways and sometimes even passed through the lines clinging to logs and flotsam.

When he caught sight of a thick, half-submerged log moving lazily along the greasy water, he didn't move. He fixed his eyes on it, straining to hear any out-of-the-ordinary sounds. There was a rustle on the other bank, and he glanced up to see his comrade rise to his knees, lifting his carbine to his shoulder.

"There was a horrible grunt," Sibeski told me, a note of desperation still audible in his tired voice, "and he pitched forward into the water. They were *behind* him," and here his voice dropped to a whisper. "And they were behind me."

Gradually Mr. Sibeski made it clear to me that he had experienced then a sickening rush of raw animal terror. Propelled by this fear, he dropped deeper into the shadows of the mangrove thicket, and slipped along the mat of roots back toward camp. Every noise he heard or made terrified him.

"I fell back," he said sadly. "I let down one of my own men, and I'll never be able to wipe that shame away."

"But," I started to say. But I knew enough about both his sense of honor and his relationship to his father not to remind him just then that the man he had wanted to help was already dead.

In the silence that followed I remembered Mr. Sibeski telling me earlier that he had gone to Vietnam to uncover the strength and courage he felt sure he had inherited from his father. In place of this reward, he seemed to have found, perhaps for a second time, disloyalty. He was horrified. No one, he felt, had discovered such a fund of fear within himself. No one felt so incompetent. No one was as homeless.

Although Mr. Sibeski looked as beaten and tired as I'd ever seen him, and surely he had come close to madness, this particular crisis seemed to be over. Perhaps his close call with paranoia had jolted him back to "reality," or perhaps getting "the main nightmare" into the open and reconnected to the rest of his life had relieved some of the pressure he so constantly lived with. What Mr. Sibeski would still not accept, he made clear to me, was hospitalization or group therapy with other veterans, but what he would consider was reading about heroes who had, more or less, gone through the kind of self-doubts and anger he was now experiencing. At my insistence, he would also try medication.

Admittedly, this was an unusual course of therapy. What I hoped Mr. Sibeski would find in the medication (but unfortunately did not) was rest and a partial release from his sense of impending doom. And what I hoped he would find in such stories as the *Odyssey, St. Brendan the Navigator,* and *Le Morte d'Arthur*—each a mysteriously persistent legend—was that good men inevitably discover very bad things in themselves but manage to turn that knowledge into wisdom rather than defeat. I knew that in Mr. Sibeski's case, the painful recognition that the essential conflict lies within would be more difficult to accept than usual because it seemed to place the blame for his distress on his psyche rather than on the war. It would be tricky to convince him that his vulnerability caused by losses in childhood and the exigencies of surviving such a vicious and morally confusing war had combined to trap him between insecurity and remorse.

Perhaps stubborn warriors, "all worn down with their dreams," as King Arthur says, can be given credit for the changes that gradually occurred in Mr. Sibeski's attitude, but I suspect it was his own persistence in reading a page or so a day of Nabokov's memoirs that began to reconnect him to his father and to memories that at last seemed to come from the heart.

With the same expressiveness that rendered his fears so vivid to me, Mr. Sibeski began to describe his early summers in Hillsdale. When he had been ten or eleven years old, he told me, he had hung out with several other boys who, like himself, spent every summer day outside. Together they fished, they whittled, they wrestled, they swam. Above all, they liked to spend a whole, long, lazy day at Silver Pond in an old green rowboat. They poled around the edge of the pond, often hidden from view by a scrim of willow branches, and they spied on the old man who wore a pouch tied to his leg and rented boats. Enemy boats they were, recognizable anywhere. Ordinary rowboats like "Becky 5" and "Bob 3," nameless little skiffs, and the broad "Jane 2" all radiated like pine needles from a narrow dock. But in the weedy shallows, out of reach and almost out of sight, lay a long, sleek canoe, and this graceful craft exerted such a powerful effect on the boys' imaginations that the mere sight of it turned them into Indians.

In the late afternoon they dressed, rubbed dirt on their hands and under their fingernails so that no one knew they'd been swimming, and hiked down to the fire station, where the men would let them slide down the pole.

Mr. Sibeski remembered hanging around with his father, too—although only on Saturdays—and these memories were drawn from the period just before his death, which earlier had seemed curiously vacant. He and his father would go to the barbershop together or the drugstore. They would walk around Hillsdale. Everyone knew the elder Mr. Sibeski, and Ivan was proud because his father looked good in his sharply creased pants and his shined shoes.

The two always stopped for an ice cream on the way home, and this event now returned to Ivan Sibeski as one of the happiest memories of his childhood. He remembered ice cream on hot days and on cold days and one time, after a visit to the dentist, his tooth hurt so much that he could not bear the cold. He felt bad then—wasting that cone—and in Vietnam he would lie in the heat, thirsty beyond description, and dream of that particular vanilla ice-cream cone and summer and Hillsdale. He wished now that he had thanked his father.

Emboldened perhaps by the return of deeper, happier memories, Mr. Sibeski finally agreed to try attending a meeting of veterans like himself. He chose a small group far from Hillsdale where only one man, Roger, knew him.

At first Mr. Sibeski took no part in the meetings. He heard the old buzzwords passing around the circle—"flashbacks," "nightmares," "fantasies of revenge"—and remained unmoved. Then one afternoon he wheeled himself into my office and announced that he was amazed at how much he'd forgotten. He had looked at photos in an album that Roger brought in, but had not been able to recognize many of the places where he had served. Even when he himself was in the picture, he had absolutely no recollection of either his surroundings or his comrades. Stories Roger told him produced the same impression—namely, that he had suffered from what could almost be called an anxiety-produced amnesia, as he had, perhaps, in the years just before and after his father's death.

However, some of Roger's stories rang true enough for Mr. Sibeski to start to correct several of his misconceptions. Not only did he begin to realize—albeit in an abstract and unemotional way—that other men besides himself felt betrayed by their commanders and by their own shortcomings but, through Roger, he also retrieved a more objective picture of himself. For one thing, Roger told him that he had not been cold to "the newer guys," nor had he been disrespectful to officers unless a man's safety was needlessly jeopardized. He learned also that he had acquired the reputation of being a good, if unusually silent, friend. He had not let everyone down.

Mr. Sibeski was also surprised to discover that each of the men in the group had fantasies of "finishing the job." For some, this meant killing every Vietcong. For others it meant driving Vietnamese civilians out of America. "It's easier if you can hate them," Mr. Sibeski explained—but for himself it meant "you have to *be* there when they need you."

Here was that theme again, I thought, rumbling forward from his father's death, through dreams of being trapped in a shower stall, to its perfect culmination in the mangrove incident. But Mr. Sibeski was already off on another topic, telling me that the group had been annoyingly unimpressed by his remorse. In fact, to Mr. Sibeski's intense embarrassment, his friend publicly proclaimed him a hero. Roger became very emotional at this point, as he told what had become for him the legend of how his life was saved by Ivan Sibeski, and this on the very night that Sibeski supposedly let everyone down.

"But you did warn us," Roger had told the group, his voice starting to crack as he remembered waking to the sounds of gunfire in the camp by the torpid canal. "Ivan, you got there in time."

The memory of shadowy forms flickering through the tentacled trees played like a film across Roger's face. The sudden attack, the shots from behind, the miraculous withdrawal. Roger cried. Mr. Sibeski's jaw tightened. Roger told him how much he admired him, loved him. Mr. Sibeski wanted to leave. He felt nothing.

From Mr. Sibeski's account, it sounded as if only Roger and a few others had been shaken by the proceedings. Yet now, in the retelling of the event, Mr. Sibeski's eyes filled with tears.

"I don't want any close friends," he said in confusion. "I don't want to worry about anyone."

"You don't want to care for family or friends and be powerless to protect them?"

"I visited with my mother a lot when I came home," he replied, jumping back in his mind some five years to when his mother had been wasting away from what he guessed was mainly disappointment. "Most days I never really knew whether she recognized me," he said softly, "but I'd sneak upstairs in the old house and . . ."

"And think of your father?"

He nodded. "And turn on the shower."

Mr. Sibeski's mother died a year after he returned from Vietnam, and he was relieved to be able to tell me that he hadn't felt a thing.

"I haven't really accepted their death, you know. I've never been to their graves."

"Why?"

"There's nothing there."

"Would you feel nothing? Or would you feel that you *have* nothing?"

"The first."

I looked at his eyes, still red from remembering Roger, and I was not so sure. Mr. Sibeski had indeed pulled away from each person who had left him through death, just as he tended to pull away from those who would care for him now. But these protective maneuvers were becoming increasingly difficult to execute. I believed he was closer than he realized to going back in his memory to the people who had left him and this time feeling the hurt and the love for himself. "Why weren't you here with *me?*" he might be able to ask if he could convince himself that he had been a good enough son or comrade to deserve some measure of love and allegiance.

That night Mr. Sibeski dreamed that he was walking alone through the countryside in Vietnam carrying a heavy pack. As he crossed each footbridge a voice called out and asked him to wait. He felt he should "befriend these familiar voices," as he put it, but he could not remember their names. He quickened his pace, but his baggage weighed him down. He knew he could not run much longer, and he was terrified. Only when he awoke in a sweat, he told me, did he realize that the voices were those of people who had died.

One could say that with this dream Mr. Sibeski set out an itinerary for himself that was not altogether different from the one I had envisioned earlier. He now suspected that it would help to remember and befriend. Such recollections, he told me, lessened the remorse. "It was not as much my fault."

His itinerary was not simple, however, and for a man such as Ivan Sibeski, who had suffered grievous losses throughout his life, it would be necessary to cycle hundreds of times through periods of attempted numbness and through periods of painful remembering. Hopefully, this cycling would slowly bring to mind both the painful emotions that had been buried because at the time there had seemed no other way of surviving them and the happy memories that had been forgotten because they were so ill-matched to present sorrows. If all this remembering went on in the presence of individuals who both understood and admired Mr. Sibeski, then through the mysterious alchemy that good listeners have long relied on, his present pain might be transformed to ordinary sadness and his old happiness set free to foster hope.

Although Mr. Sibeski had survived nearly a year of sobriety and breasted what were probably the strongest tides of returning memories, he was still "on the edge" when it came time for me to leave his section of Mountain Valley. Predictably, my departure stirred up memories of being abandoned, and his first reaction was to talk of withdrawing from therapy and the veterans' group. We had a tough month, and I knew it would be hard to leave him.

In our last sessions I found myself doing more of the talking than usual. It was my last chance to bully some hope into him and to tell him how amazed I was by his ability to endure months of emotional agony without going crazy. I wanted him to know that I would always think of him as the point man, as the lonely hunter or explorer who "goes before." In my attempt to bundle all these good wishes into his arms, I found myself telling Mr. Sibeski about a curious assortment of characters that included King Arthur, William James, and my mother. I told him of trips I had taken and of fears I had met. Finally I sat back, feeling a little peculiar for so insistently reversing the usual direction of conversation.

Tactfully, gracefully, Mr. Sibeski picked up the theme of my stories. He had been wheeling along the back roads that very afternoon, he told me, when he spotted a dead fox outside one of the hospital gates. He stopped then and thought for a long time about the dead and how they should be honored. Picking up a stick, he managed to move the scrawny animal, not just off the road but into the woods.

I did not interpret. Instead, I passed back to him a memory I had of finding a near-dead opossum at the side of the road, an animal who could move nothing save his eyes. And a curious thing happened. Quite abruptly we understood that we had connected with each other through Mr. Sibeski's ability to love the farms around Hillsdale. He had searched for solitary comfort among the cornfields, but he had returned each week to tell me of his travels.

"And now, Mr. Sibeski," I said, "your woods with their squirrels and foxes are in some measure my woods, and my near-dead 'possum is your 'possum."

He smiled, and for a moment or two I had the curious impression that with this exhange of expiring animals—of memories, of ways of seeing the world—we had concluded some kind of pact.

That was the last I saw of Mr. Sibeski. We said our good-byes formally, and I watched his now familiar figure roll down the hall to the handicapped exit. He disappeared into the early-autumn sun.

I do not know how this unusual man has fared, only that he is still alive and that he has chosen not to return to Mountain Valley Hospital for whatever it is that psychologists earnestly try to do there. Yet in my mind's eye I sometimes see him rolling effortlessly along country roads, through patches of dappled shade and out into sunlit fields. I picture him gliding through those old farmlands, his golden ponytail flying out behind. Above, the sky is a deep, clear blue, and at his side fields of goldenrod blaze with monarch butterflies. I choose to believe that, like those butterflies, which may or may not complete their long migration to Mexico, he too has drifted the first few feet toward another spring.

Conclusion:
In Search of a Usable Past

To be understood deeply and intelligently and to be treasured is a combination that deflects the course of any life. Everything else is stuff.

JUDITH HORGAN

On a gray day last spring, I revisited that portion of Mountain Valley Hospital that I have called Ward 9-2-D. I was after the answers to ambitious questions that day. I wanted to know what was helpful about remembering, both the remembering that goes on in therapy, where the past is rewoven with the present, and the remembering that goes on later, when the therapist, or any person who understood so well, is gone.

Having driven past the battered CHOOSE 'N' CUT Christmas tree sign, I turned onto High Street and a minute later jounced over the speed bumps at the entrance to the hospital grounds. In spite of the drizzle, men from the greenhouse bent over the flower beds that circled the guardhouse. I wondered if Dallas Grey was among them, crouching over the private pit that figured so prominently in his delusions of torture. Before me the steep-roofed buildings of the hospital climbed partway up the valley, and beyond I could sense rather than see the darkness of wet pines. Every feature was familiar, yet as I drove past the clinics and acute wards and headed toward Building 9 at the back of the grounds, I began to feel out of place. I had not been a regular participant on 9-2-D for over two years.

Driving on up the hill to the right, I parked by Building 9 and walked onto the ward just as the patients came straggling back for "noon meds."

"Mr. Mark," I said, walking up behind the courtly gentleman who sometimes confused himself with Robert E. Lee.

"Ahh Doctor . . . , Dr. Baur. Let me tell you, it's a shame. There is only a very little bit of love left in this world. Very little.

"Say," he continued, apparently remembering something more about me than my name. "Do you remember promising me a good book?"

"Yes I do, Mr. Mark. Have you decided which book you would like?"

"Why I would like a short book," he answered thoughtfully. "Short and concise. That's for me."

Chatting together as if no time had elapsed since my departure, Mr. Mark and I strolled into the dayroom. He carried on as always about the frustrations of life, especially for a gentleman, especially for "a tall man and a good man." It was the same description he had used for himself years before.

Mr. Mountbank, who had lost his sister, nodded agreeably as he paced back and forth. Others smiled. The man with the beautiful slanted eyes did not recognize me at all. Another paused in his praying long enough to wave.

Although many patients acted as if I'd been away for two weeks rather than two years, the few who acknowledged the passage of time did so by associating me with some incident from the past rather than by telling me how they had fared, or asking me how I had done. It was as if their lives turned in place rather than progressing in any small or ordinary way.

"You were the one with the brown dog," whispered a small man as he slipped by me.

And another, waggling his cigarette-stained finger, said rather accusingly, "You worked here when Mary Frances was here. After Jean. Before Gretchen. You left 9-2-D. Yes, you did."

With these patients, I too reached backward rather than forward for connections.

"Remember when you got that brass kaleidoscope?" I asked one.

"Remember when you made a mask for Halloween?"

With the staff, however, the present was more intriguing than the past, and in a variety of ways we asked each other how things were going now. Has So-and-so finished her new house? Did she kick her lazy son out? Who has gotten married or divorced?

And when I talked with the ward psychologist about the patients, I again wanted to be brought up to date. How had the patients changed? More than half had improved enough, he told me, to live more independently. Some, like the grandiose Ivana Goldman, were still in the hospital but were now spending their weekdays at a community center in Hillsdale. Others, like Mr. Clauson, with the green plums, were living in foster homes. And several, among them the devout patient who spoke with God about smoking and Dallas Grey who carried with him memories of Dr. Sweetheart, had gone back and forth between foster homes and hospital. Many, of course, were still on 9-2-D.

"And Mr. Nouvelle?" I finally asked. "How's he doing?"

"Well," said the psychologist somewhat hesitantly. "Mr. Nouvelle met our new criteria for minimal progress."

"Which means?" I asked, surprised by the unfamiliar term and the implication that he was headed for discharge.

"Which means he's no longer part of this program. He's been sent to another ward. You see, every month we review the patients' progress, and if we feel . . ."

As my former supervisor explained the changes that had occurred since my departure, the distant feeling I'd had on approaching Building 9 returned, and I realized quite abruptly that I too was out of "the program." I was no longer a member of this staff. I was simply a visitor.

"And after you left he never did as well again," the psychologist was saying. "His behaviors are so unacceptable in the community. You know the uh-uh-uh,"—and here he gingerly imitated Mr. Nouvelle's sucking motions. "You might say that you can dress him up, but you can't take him out. . . . He slipped back after you left."

Later that afternoon I headed for Building 4 to discover, if I could, what Mr. Nouvelle had slipped back into. I had learned only that he was on a back ward where he was still expected to trim his nails and brush his teeth, for example, but where he was no longer required to line up for daily checks on personal hygiene or earn points for extra privileges. Nor did he have to attend "communications group" to learn how to speak or therapy sessions to teach an intern how to listen. He had been let out to pasture again, and I wondered whether the lowered expectations would be a relief for him or feel like further abandonment. I wondered too if I would recognize myself in his memories, or if I had already been changed into one of those elusive goat or chipmunk ladies who tormented him by turning into strangers.

As I approached Building 4, I spotted a small, stooped man in brown clothes coming toward me and recognized a thinner, older-looking Mr. Nouvelle. He had new frames for his glasses, which sat crookedly on his face, and on the front of his shirt he wore an enormous green pin in the shape of a lettuce leaf, apparently an advertisement for a local salad bar. As usual, he stared intently at the ground as he walked. Also as usual, he seemed wrapped in his own thoughts.

"Mr. Nouvelle," I said, smiling.

There followed several moments of confusion as the Dinosaur Man stared at me, whipped out a detached dick, threw it away, cleared his throat, and finally cried.

"How have you been?" I asked, as the tears rolled down his face. "You're thin. You're not eating."

"You have been away for a billion years," he said at last, "and I have missed our companionship."

Mr. Nouvelle and I spent the next twenty minutes together in the Annex drinking sparkling water—an *apéritif*, he called it. We sat on either side of a Formica table richly patterned with cigarette burns, and at our elbows food machines hummed and blinked. Patients I knew and many I didn't shuffled past. Against this familiar backdrop Mr. Nouvelle's memories of the time we had spent together returned in chunks, and although I cannot remember all he said, I do recall the sense of pressure that drove us both to try to cover all topics of importance simultaneously.

"Do you still have a vine-covered cottage waiting for me? Did we get married?" he asked, straining to recall the nature of our connection. "No, wait," he continued, "you were my dinosaur daughter, weren't you? Yes."

Once reconnected to his former role, Mr. Nouvelle rattled on for a few minutes about dinosaurs, families, and teachers.

"Do you remember the garden?" I asked.

"Our garden," he corrected.

"And what did we plant there?"

"Corn?"

"No, not corn."

"Squash?"

"No, no, you're going mushy in your squash. What did we plant?"

"Tomatoes."

"Beans, Mr. Nouvelle, beans."

"On the tepee poles," he chimed in, the memory of our garden finally separating itself from those of all the other gardens he had worked in before. "But the lettuce didn't do very well."

"Indeed it did not," I replied and wondered why it seemed so important and so wonderful that we should both reclaim those scraggly, dried-out seedlings and those hot summer days.

Mr. Nouvelle went on to talk about chapel. He was disturbed

by voices there and sometimes walked out, although he wasn't sure whether that was the best thing to do. In a similar vein, many of the things we discussed were strange, but, given what I knew about him, they all made sense. In fact, for the first time since I had met him nearly three years before, Mr. Nouvelle did not interrupt our conversation every three or four minutes to dodge behind a thicket of incomprehensible babble.

"So what do you do all day?" I asked. "Still go to OT?"

"Oh yes . . . , I mean no. Not anymore. I roam all over the hospital."

He paused, apparently reexamining my question from another angle. "But I have a job," he said earnestly. "I'm a guard in this prison, you know. Every morning I take the men from 4-1-B to the mess hall in the shipyard. Yes, and I arrange for their valet service. And I cook for them. I am a culinary expert now, a *vontage.*"

"*Ah, mon cher monsieur,*" I replied, "an intoxicating life."

"No," he answered, smiling at this familiar silly business, "lonely."

"And memories? Do they comfort you?"

"Uhh . . . , well, they say I have a long-term problem," he answered, probably referring to his long-term memory and having trouble as always changing from one topic to another. "I can't remember what I want. I mean, I keep getting the wrong memories."

Only a few mental illnesses are described in terms of absent or mistaken memories, but Mr. Nouvelle's assertion that his mind gave him the wrong memories was an interesting way of looking at emotional distress and at the work I had done throughout Mountain Valley. When I began this work, I was far less concerned with memory, either with the conscious recollections commonly called memories or with the silent, "forgotten" recollections that Freud realized play on like deep music in the mind. Although I knew that therapy involves gathering background information, I thought that chronic patients especially would feel so cut off from their families and from the outside world that they would wish to concentrate on present problems. I also assumed that, because they were such unreliable historians, it would make no sense for me to examine their early lives. Finally, I believed that any small improvement I could make in the quality of their present lives would not rely directly on anything in their pasts, forgotten or remembered. In all this I was wrong.

On my first day on 9-2-D, I had not been on the ward an hour before Mr. Mark peered down at me from under his bushy eyebrows and asked, "Do you want my life cold turkey on a plate?" And I had not been on the ward a week before I began to suspect that delusional histories differ mainly in degree, not in kind, from the edited and reedited accounts we all construct. That personal histories form an essential, but curiously flexible prologue to the future took longer for me to understand.

In any case, I was so astonished by the stories offered willingly by the patients that after some months I had many of the patients on 9-2-D writing or dictating or dreaming their autobiographies. We were in search of a usable past, I told them, an account that was ordinary enough to be understood by others, clear enough to explain why a person felt the way he did, and positive enough to sustain some measure of self-esteem. But why should these particular qualities be important for a personal history? And why should they have to be discovered in the past? Why not settle for a usable present?

First to the qualities that characterize a usable past—accuracy, organization, and positive recollections. Memories are remarkably and, I now believe, necessarily flexible, but they do need to be accurate enough to be understood by others if an individual is to be a part of a community. A cow pasture, for example, may be recalled as a meadow or a grassland but not as a swamp full of dinosaurs, and part of Mr. Nouvelle's problem with "wrong memories" was that when he told a story, other people did not believe him and would not listen.

Memories can be inaccurate in another way, namely, they can

fail to carry the added information which identifies them as coming from the mind, like dreams, or from the outside, like personal experience. I had used my somewhat frustrating say-it, think-it reality-monitoring test to confirm that this part of memory is more frequently compromised among schizophrenics than among most other people. The consequence, as Lloyd Bartlett knew too well, is the frequent mistaking of thoughts for experience, and this in turn made patients like him wary of conversing for fear they would reveal their illness. Even Wanda McGowan was frequently misunderstood because of the ease with which she believed her own flamboyant exaggerations.

To my knowledge, Mr. Nouvelle was never particularly bothered by what others saw as the inaccuracy of his memory, but he did complain of a disorganization which I commonly encountered among chronic schizophrenics. "I do not have a memory where things stay put," he said, and indeed he had a terrible time keeping one experience from leaking into all the others. He might talk for a minute or two about the time he planted a pear tree, for example, but fairly soon the story would be infiltrated by fragments from other times and topics. Often a story would be derailed altogether and go wandering off to a logging camp or to God the Father.

The silent Mr. O'Reilly's memories were unorganized rather than disorganized. Perhaps because he had grown up in an unusually quiet family, whose members tried to control their feelings with a rigorous silence, he had not cultivated the habit of telling stories or even of arranging his experience in storylike memories. Isolated memories, I knew, are more difficult to recall than stories, and Mr. O'Reilly retained remarkably little from his past. Nor did he want to, for few of his past experiences would support the fiction that his only desires in this world were to be absolutely calm and silent. Neither Mr. O'Reilly's unorganized memories nor the Dinosaur Man's disorganized ones could do one of the things that adequate memories are supposed to do—explain to a person why he believes what he believes and feels the way he feels.

The third problem routinely encountered at Mountain Valley was the lack of positive elements—such as love, respect, or appreciation—in the patients' memories, and without these they were hard-pressed to sustain an adequate self-image. Both Dallas Grey's and Ivan Sibeski's memories were strikingly bereft of sustained happiness. As children, neither had grown accustomed to being consistently appreciated, and neither found it easy even to register the compliments paid them as adults. Over and over I pointed out their aptitudes, but my compliments did not seem to stick unless I prodded these men into reclaiming scraps of appreciation from the past as well. It was as if no belief could exist without a foundation, as if each man were saying, "I can only be what I have always been."

"Your father must have gotten great pleasure from showing you off in town," I mused aloud to Mr. Sibeski. Or to Dallas Grey, "Dr. Sweetheart must have liked you a lot to talk with you every day. You must have made him feel good."

So as I tried to cultivate the kind of history I am calling a usable past, I came up against memories so inaccurate that they hampered communication, recollections so muddled that the present unfolded from nothing and made no sense, and reminiscence so bleak that the rememberer could not believe himself worthy of esteem. With "wrong memories" like these, Wanda McGowan could chain herself in place for life and Mr. Nouvelle cut himself adrift from the rest of the world.

Was the best approach, then, to teach accuracy, organization, and positive thinking—assuming that such could be done—or was it preferable to take on the vastly more ambitious task of revising the memories that had already been stored in my patients' minds? To say yes to the second proposition would be to argue that a person's problems cannot be ameliorated unless his very identity is modified, which of course means changing his past. With some other therapists, especially Adlerians and certain of the cognitive therapists, I have come to believe in this quite preposterous-sounding idea. Specifically, I now believe that, without realizing it, all of us revise our past whenever we change our present, and that this dual process is at the center of therapy and of ordinary development as well. I further believe that one *must* change both the past and the present, for the two work reciprocally on each other in deeper ways than are commonly realized.

We know now that individuals use memory the way scientists use data, which is to say that people scan their past, as well as their present, for information that will confirm what they already know or strongly suspect. At the same time, what they already know and expect significantly influences what they will see and remember. In oversimplified terms, what we remember of the past molds the present, while what we are concerned with in the present shapes our memory of the past. This is a fine homeostatic process, and it tends to keep identities running true to form. Worriers remain worriers. Optimists remain optimists.

But identities change nevertheless. The manipulative woman mellows, the grandiose woodsman becomes an apprehensive mental patient. Because such individuals now respond to situations in a different way, must we infer that their memories have somehow changed? Would they describe different childhoods depending on their current point of view?

The noted psychoanalyst Alfred Adler said yes. He believed that he could see how the present and past work on each other by observing how the earliest memories of his patients changed as the individuals themselves changed. He noted that when he asked a person for the first experiences he could remember, the individual seemed to be saying with his response, "See? Even as a small child life has been like this for me." If life then changed for a person in an important way, Adler believed that this individual would remember a different set of events or put a different twist on the same events in order to bring the past in line with his present feelings. The advantage of such a system to the individual is that it gives him a steady, confident feeling that he has always been more or less the same kind of person he is now. Each of his beliefs has a history as long as his memory, and he is unshakable. The disadvantage is that it is difficult to change from one unshakable position to another.

When I first asked Mr. Nouvelle for his earliest memory, the Dinosaur Man was at his most elusive.

"I was eighteen months old," he said dreamily. "I slept in my parents' room and I saw them making love. I saw her give my father a hand job and I said, 'I can do better than that,' so I gave him a blow job. It's hard the first time you get caught," he continued, "but you just agree with them and say, 'Yes, I'm eating my father. He likes it. It's a good thing to do.' Then they let you alone."

Some months later I again asked Mr. Nouvelle for the earliest event he could remember. This time he described picking beans as a little boy with his father.

"My father used to say, 'You're missing all of them.' Could it be that he didn't understand that those beans didn't want to be picked? He was a simpleton just like me. Or maybe it didn't mean anything."

I would not want to claim that Mr. Nouvelle's bean-picking memory is so much more realistic or so much "healthier" than his fellatio memory that the progression reflects an irrefutable improvement in this man's mental health. I would say, however, that the second memory is less delusional and easier to understand. This change alone suggests that Mr. Nouvelle has become less guarded and more willing to communicate the actual events of his life.

By comparison, Dallas Grey's earliest memories never deviated from themes of chaos and danger. "It was lightning and heat wave," he told me when I asked for his earliest recollection. "I was just waiting for the World War to get over. I was about four or five or four or three years old and my mother said, 'It's always this way in wartime. Thunderstorms and clouds.' She explained the whole thing and said, 'That's war.' I said, 'Oh, it didn't bother me, a bad one rocking the house.' I thought we were getting a little piece of the war, and they were going to put us first-graders out there to go get 'em."

On another occasion Mr. Grey claimed to remember his own breech birth, a bloody affair in which everyone was hurt, including the family dog. Although the small, retiring Mr. Grey recently spent nearly a year out of the hospital, and thus showed himself better able than Mr. Nouvelle to adapt to a more demanding and hopefully more rewarding set of circumstances, his earliest memories were consistently painful and confused. There was no easily detectable progression that suggested that he felt differently about himself or the rest of the world.

Assuming for a moment that all recollections, not just earliest memories, are flexible constructions, and that individuals feel a strong but unconscious need to modify them in order to justify their present attitudes, it becomes possible to see why therapy needs to work simultaneously on past and present. A therapist who wishes to be an effective agent of change must tinker with the vast structure of recollection so that new attitudes and new ways of dealing with people seem to spring from deep in the past—seem almost inevitable.

"I've always wanted to leave the hospital," murmurs a patient on the eve of his departure—a patient who several years before was unwilling even to consider the idea of leaving. But someone has helped him find faint traces of independent yearnings in his past, and now he leaves the hospital supported by years of his own desiring.

In a similar manner, individuals like Mr. O'Reilly and Ivan Sibeski needed to rebuild their histories to support new self-esteem and understanding. In reviving memories of both strength and weakness, acceptance and rejection, I had hoped each would discover compelling examples of his own goodness and would also feel again the sadness and emptiness that could at least partly explain the difficulty each had experienced in staying with the wife, parents, or comrades he had loved. These men needed to remember that they themselves had not received the abundance of love and support that enables a person to give these gifts freely and easily to others later on.

Of course, to be modified, a memory must be brought into consciousness, and it is no easy task to remember what you have needed very badly to forget. For years Mr. Sibeski had survived the loss of his parents by "forgetting" how much he loved them, and at the age of thirty-nine to pry loose from memory repressed sensations of intense affection was to reopen grievous wounds. In a similar fashion, Mr. O'Reilly controlled whatever feelings of remorse he had by "forgetting" that throughout his life he had fairly glowed with the desire to drink and swear and make more noise than was ever tolerated in his childhood home. And the Dinosaur Man had needed more forgetting or repressing than both these men combined. To hold together the fragments of his battered identity, he needed to disavow his experience almost entirely and forget that he had been treated as a replacement for another child, been born to a tired mother and a father distracted by pain, and been convinced that "it was all up to me. And I failed."

I now believe that one cannot remember these critical events with their overpowering feelings unless one has changed, but that one cannot change unless enough of the past is revived and reinterpreted to provide a new perspective on the present. This is indeed a catch-22 situation. If Mr. Sibeski wished to suffer less remorse, for example, he needed to endure the painful recollection of loving and being parted from his parents. But when I first met him he was too lonely and beset by remorse to sustain additional pain. In other words, he could not move forward without lowering his defenses, and it was precisely this that he could not afford to do. He was stuck.

This is a common kind of a problem, and, depending on the school of thought that a therapist subscribes to, there are different ways to try to break the deadlock. If the impasse is believed to be psychological, then the troubled individual may be helped to clarify and then modify his thinking, his actions, and/or his feelings. (These three realms correspond roughly to cognitive, behavioral, and emotive therapies. Clinicians using each expect that a change in one aspect of functioning will lead to changes in the other two.) If the problem is considered primarily physiological, then medication is prescribed, and, again, it is hoped that this biochemical change will be followed by new ways of thinking, acting, and feeling. In terms of memory and a usable past, I was attempting to break the deadlock by serving for a time as an auxiliary memory, a process that falls generally within the realm of cognitive therapy.

"I feel like an old man," Mr. Nouvelle once said with disgust after he had lost his balance in the garden and fallen on a marigold plant. "I look old."

"But Mr. Nouvelle," I replied, deciding in this instance to hand him back one of his own memories rather than explore his feelings about age, "just last week you told me that you looked like a god. Remember? We were at the picnic table and you said you'd seen yourself with big, *big* eyes and a terrific build."

Mr. Nouvelle looked blank.

"You said you were tan like the man in the television commercial who falls into the pool."

"Oh yes," he finally agreed, brightening. "And I asked you if that is the way women like a man to be."

"And *I* said—" and here we both began to laugh.

Essentially I was encouraging the Dinosaur Man to temper his feelings by asking his own recollections for help, and I could do this because I had collected, held, and clarified thousands of his memories. Some I produced when his self-image needed support. Some I gently moved from private imagery—"my goat-wife"—toward consensual reality—"the woman in the gym." And some I organized into accounts that might begin to explain his raging feelings.

In a similar manner, when Mr. Nouvelle thought himself powerless, I reminded him of how he had affected others. And when he lost his train of thought, I brought him back, ready or not.

"But the problem you just mentioned. You said your wives were unhappy because—"

"Well, they've got you wired today so you remember everything I say," he snapped.

And, indeed, I tried to remember everything he said that carried with it any trace of heartfelt feeling. I tried to shore up the memories that made him feel like a good person, and I tried to clarify those that made him feel bad or powerless. I stored. I sorted. I analyzed. I resorted. But most of all I brought Mr. Nouvelle's cascading memories together as if I were trying with all my strength to create a community of selves where only fragments had been before. I was the *hablador*, the storyteller who kept dinosaurs,

194

soldiers, and sophisticated men connected in the jungle of his mind.

It would be nice to report that my efforts to modify the problems of patients like Mr. Nouvelle and to root these changes in the past succeeded in a dramatic and visible way, but by and large what changes we managed were subtle. For example, during my time on 9-2-D, Dallas Grey's memories of Dr. Sweetheart were refreshed and reinforced, and with them Mr. Grey's confidence in himself. Although I never figured out what was going on in this man's mind, apparently something happened that helped him to live outside the hospital for the first time in many years, albeit for a limited time. When I think of Mr. Grey (who chose his own pseudonym by asking to be called Stella Dallas or Zane Grey), I think of a carved wooden box, the kind with a false bottom and a secret drawer that Yankee seamen made on long voyages. I asked myself if there were anything I could do to the outside of such a box—and that is all I had access to—that would influence the inside, but Dallas Grey very quietly suggested that I was asking too many questions.

Maybe you'll get through to me . . . , his shy, buck-toothed smile seemed to say.

And maybe I won't, I added to myself, and wondered why so many of us on the staff slipped toward the unproductive idea that we could only appreciate the patients we could understand or, worse, only appreciate the ones we could influence. Tiny, molelike Dallas. My guess is that no one after Dr. Sweetheart will ever understand his life very well, or significantly alter its course.

"That's the way it goes, Doctor," I can imagine the Super Dr. Sweetheart saying.

On the face of it, Ivan Sibeski was a great deal easier to understand than Dallas Grey, yet his life too was marked by secrecy. I remember how surprised I felt when I learned from a psychiatrist, who had seen Mr. Sibeski only once for medication, that my patient had encountered an old high school girlfriend. Why hadn't he told me? I would have asked a dozen questions.

And that, of course, goes a long way toward explaining why he *hadn't* told me.

In spite of Mr. Sibeski's monumental reticence, we worked hard together—miracle enough—and for some reason the memory that I associate above all with him is the peculiar way in which we sometimes shared the burden of his recollections from Vietnam. He did not want to remember these episodes, much less relate them, for the feelings they uncovered were grindingly painful. Added to this was his concern that the memories of young men dying would upset me. Of course they upset me. They had me groping for Kleenex. They had me crying in my car on the way home.

"And why not?" I would fairly shout at him. "You tell me about a nineteen-year-old dying or the sounds that a man makes when he is run through with a bayonet, and I'm not supposed to feel horrible? I *hate* it. Keep talking." Mr. Sibeski did keep talking, but he never exactly understood why I was willing to feel the feelings while he said the words. What he did seem to understand from my peculiar response, however, was that the reactions he expressed only in nightmares were less cowardly than he'd first imagined. Perhaps it wasn't always wrong to acknowledge feelings of pain and fear.

And what of the silent Mr. O'Reilly, who, like Mr. Sibeski, has not chosen to continue therapy? I can still see his embarrassed grin and apologetic shrug as he sat silently in the corner. This man did not have the faintest idea of how therapy is supposed to proceed, but, to care for his ailing wife, he tolerated the uncomfortable world of words and feelings week after week. Better than anyone I have ever met, Mr. O'Reilly balanced himself between trust and personal dignity. He gave to a person from another world the secrets of a strange life, and I, increasingly impressed by his bravery, strove to exceed my usual limits of understanding. For the fifty minutes each week that I was with Mr. O'Reilly, he was a terrific person and I was a wonderful therapist. We shared the prize.

And what was the prize I hoped to share with Mr. Nouvelle?

Sometimes on the long drives home from Mountain Valley I used to imagine possible cures. I never pictured him in a "vine-covered cottage," as he used to say, for his illness of thirty-seven years had removed him so completely from society and from the usual experiences of growing up that, even if his schizophrenia were suddenly to disappear, he would not know enough about himself or the world to succeed at either love or work. Nor did I picture the Dinosaur Man sitting on the stoop of a foster home in Hillsdale, nor yet returning north to the woods and farmlands of his youth to be cared for by a family whose memories had hardened around the embarrassment and frustration he had caused them.

But occasionally I allowed myself the luxury of imagining Mr. Nouvelle in a rambling house at the back of the hospital or perhaps on the grounds of a monastery somewhere. There he might live, with a dozen or so patients like himself and several staff members in what is sometimes called a therapeutic household. He and his comrades would go to work every day, planting a garden or collecting eggs from under the chickens he still dreams about at night. I realized that he might be captured for hours by the smell of chopped straw and have to be reminded to pick up his hoe, or he might alarm passersby by fondling a field full of cantaloupes. But, given time, he could plant and harvest. I had seen him do it. And while I was fantasizing, I also wished a Dr. Sweetheart into Mr. Nouvelle's life, a person who would talk to him or fly past him every day for a million years. Mr. Nouvelle would connect. I'd seen him do that also.

And I hoped too that someone would give to him, and patients like him, the serious job of teaching young clinicians what it is like to be schizophrenic. No one can communicate the confusion and agony of this illness with so little self-pity as Maurice Nouvelle, and no one can illustrate the desperate protection of delusions with such vividness. More important than these useful lessons, however, is Mr. Nouvelle's unparalleled ability to blur the distinction between sanity and madness. Surely this man is mad. His thoughts are tangled, his crumbling memory choked with delusions, and his ability to care for himself that of a small child. Yet beneath all these disabilities he yearns as keenly as anyone for love and esteem. His feelings are sane, even though the rest of him wavers back and forth across the line that divides "them" from "us."

One afternoon Mr. Nouvelle and I stood under a porch and watched a spring rain beat on the green grass of the ball field. Agitated, Mr. Nouvelle rattled on about the pizza served at lunch, which had turned into dead meat on his plate. Howitzer Bombardier had flown into a murderous rage and wanted to shoot everyone in the dining hall but was not able to, for reasons I could not follow.

"Let's take a walk," I suggested, to change the topic, and I pretended to move into the downpour.

"Then they'd really lock me up," he replied with a chuckle, suddenly swerving back into my world.

"And would they lock me up too?"

"Of course not. They know the difference."

A few moments later, he added, "And so do we."

I was astonished as always by his understanding, and by his uncanny ability to keep me off-balance. He fostered in me an uncertainty as profound as my fascination. And this was the Dinosaur Man's gift to those fortunate enough to know him. He erased the lines and boundaries. He slyly suggested that we would be wise to hold on to uncertainty. He astonished us all. In my experience, only the Grand Canyon is as improbable as Mr. Nouvelle.

And so at the end of that gray day on the back wards of Mountain Valley, I walked toward Building 4 to say good-bye to a sophisticated man or to babble incoherently with an indooblecated bombardier. In my mind I returned to the questions I had brought with me. Why had I encouraged the Dinosaur Man and my other patients to go back into their lives to feel again the love, which by and large they had lost, and to call out again in hurt and anger? Because, I said to myself, and with more confidence than I had felt before, because that is how I understood them best, and how I engaged their entire lives in the service of their present welfare. Also, I had learned that my patients could not believe in love—whether it came from me or from them—that was based on anything other than deep understanding. On the ward and in the clinic they watched me travel through their pasts, reinterpreting what I found there in the light of my different and more benign experience. They watched me find treasure, and to some extent they copied my explorations and found a treasure in themselves.

I had asked also about the remembering that may go on, as it sporadically does in Mr. Grey's mind, when a person like Dr. Sweetheart has gone or when the one who understood so well has died. Even with a map of heaven, how hard a person must struggle to find a way to keep the remembered dialogue of love alive. How difficult I had found that to be myself. And how much harder these acts of faith must be for an individual whose brain turns an ordinary week into a hundred years and people into dinosaurs.

In one of his saddest moments, as Mr. Nouvelle was trying to accept my departure from 9-2-D, I remembered him saying to me, "I am afraid everything will be over and I won't have had anything. Does a dinosaur, I mean a dinosaur's daughter, understand that?"

At the time I understood him to be saying that he was afraid that those ordinary and often impossible dreams of love and happiness would never come true for him, but now I realized that there was a second threat to his tenuous hope for well-being. With his irreparably disorganized memory, "everything"—or what little he got—might be over and he wouldn't have *remembered* anything. Perhaps all the exploring we had done together of his past and all the sightings we had made of Mountain Valley's dinosaurs had not produced for him a memorable account. How then could he profit from either the self-understanding I had tried to promote or the self-esteem I had tried to foster? There is no answer to this question. From time to time Mr. Nouvelle may think of the garden behind the abandoned greenhouse, or the beans on their tepee poles, and perhaps these thoughts will trigger some happy memories left in his heart from long ago. Such memories may comfort him and may even make it easier for him to see whatever affection and appreciation there is around him in this hospital which is his home.

199

CONCLUSION: IN SEARCH OF A USABLE PAST

* * *

The last time I saw the Dinosaur Man it was nearly autumn again in Mountain Valley. The dinosaurs who had been adrift in the meadows all summer long were beginning to move toward the shelter of Building 9. They moved more slowly, I thought, and seemed more preoccupied than ever with their private thoughts. The small father dinosaur told me in his distracted way that his daughter had left his end of the valley—perhaps she had gone away to school again—but that like all good daughters she would not forget her father. She would visit sometimes, and she would have a Mass said for him in honor of St. Dymphna. That, at any rate, is what the Dinosaur Man said he remembers of me, and this is what I remember of him. They say that what is remembered goes on living and can happen again.

AFTERWORD AND ACKNOWLEDGMENTS

In the middle of my tenure on Ward 9-2-D, I spent part of a warm May afternoon spying on dinosaurs with Mr. Nouvelle. We had been sitting together on the concrete veranda of Building 9, gazing at the cut fields across the road, when Mr. Nouvelle started talking about what I guessed was a scene from his rural childhood. At first, he rambled on incomprehensibly about chicken wattles, beans that didn't want to be picked, and a tractor that God the Father taught him, or at least allowed him, to drive.

"Tell me what you see out there in the field," I suggested, and, as I had hoped, my request prompted Mr. Nouvelle to cut through some of his chronic confusion. He told me then that pumpkins were loaded onto a pickup truck and driven into the fields, where "horses and the dinosaur images of you and me and your mother are grazing. The horses crack the pumpkins open with their front hooves so they can chew them."

"And the dinosaurs?" I asked, joining him in his imaginary world. "Do they crack the pumpkins open with their big feet?"

"Well . . . ," the Dinosaur Man replied slowly, seeming to

201

teeter for a moment between the logic of my world and the brilliant fantasy of his own, "they could . . . , but they are so big that they eat them whole like grapes. Do you see them out there now munching on grapes?"

It was my turn to teeter, and in the warm sun with the smell of freshly cut grass blowing in from the fields, it was easy to imagine a lumbering dinosaur family browsing on pumpkins, munching on golden grapes.

"Hmm," I answered, and because it was one of those rare and peaceful moments at Mountain Valley, my answer was apparently sufficient.

Later that afternoon, I left Mr. Nouvelle and the other patients on Ward 9-2-D, and on the way home I stopped at a small gallery in a white farmhouse where an exhibit of collages, objects, and boxes had just opened. Still picturing dinosaurs munching on pumpkins, I walked into a roomful of polished conundrums. In front of me were boxes made of lustrous walnut and mahogany, and in each were arcane arrangements of the forgotten, the broken, and the mismatched. There were tarot cards and whitened bones, old maps and the heads of small china dolls. One dark pine box had been divided into tiny compartments, each of which held a songbird's egg. In front of this speckled wall, two plastic pigs were having tea. In another box, a slant-eyed baby doll sat holding a miniature poster on which was a picture of its mother.

Why, I'm back on the ward, I thought. I recognize every one of these improbable arrangements.

But there was an agreeable difference. Somehow the artist, whom I had never met and who I assumed had no special knowledge of mental illness, had seen through the tangled impediments which, I feel, ordinarily obscure the dark and puzzling questions that encircle many lives. In one box, for example, which in my mind I immediately titled "Dreams of the Dinosaur Man," I could all but read off the questions that I had begun to formulate with Mr. Nouvelle. Was this small box with its decorated door telling me a story about opening up or closing down? Did its battered bluebird, half out of the box, symbolize breaking free or remaining trapped? And the small skull? The excluded but still-attached heart? The tethered float? Looking at this box, I felt again the intense ambiguity that I experienced in the presence of the Dinosaur Man, and I sensed again, in the apparently irrational but curiously satisfying juxtaposition of objects, this patient's indomitable harmony. Like the artist's, my goal was to see beyond both the delusional dilemmas that my patients posed for themselves and the apparently senseless monologues of torture and seduction that they created in response. Sometimes, beneath all their breaking and forgetting, mismatching and mislabeling, I thought I could see the person who still struggled to live a brave and loving life.

Thus I wish to thank Domenic Cimino, whose work, moving parallel to my own in many ways, has encouraged me to put my observations into words. Claudine Marquet organized the original exhibit, and I am grateful to her as well. Thanks of a different nature I happily extend to my mentor and friend Dr. S. O. Watson and to the warmhearted Dr. Kevin Flynn. The manuscript has been read by the majority of counselors and clinicians at the Massachusetts Rehabilitation Commission's Harbor Area Office and by my friends Betty Fuller, Pam Peters, and Lynn Forbes. Thanks also to a fine Irish storyteller, Dr. Bernie O'Brien, to Dr. Bill Hallstein, whose rambunctious thinking gleefully defies convention, and to my mother, Louisa Baur. Kathy Banks at HarperCollins and Miriam Altshuler at Russell & Volkening gave me much valuable help.

When I left one of the clinics in Hillsdale, the patients in my therapy group made a large and somewhat unconventionally worded card for me. I would like to return their good wishes and say back to all of them, "Good-bye and go lucky, you too!"